A Theory of Grocery Shopping

A Theory of Grocery Shopping

Food, Choice and Conflict

Shelley L. Koch

London · New York

English edition
First published in 2012 by
Berg
Editorial offices:
50 Bedford Square, London WC1B 3DP, UK
175 Fifth Avenue, New York, NY 10010, USA

Berg is an imprint of Bloomsbury Publishing Plc.

Library of Congress Cataloging-in-Publication Data

A catalogue record for this book is available from the Library of Congress.

British Library Cataloguing-in-Publication Data

A catalogue record for this book is available from the British Library.

ISBN 978 0 85785 150 5 (Cloth)
978 0 85785 151 2 (Paper)
e-ISBN 978 0 85785 153 6 (individual)

Typeset by Apex CoVantage, LLC, Madison, WI, USA.
Printed in the UK by the MPG Books Group

www.bergpublishers.com

To my family, with love.

Contents

Acknowledgments   ix

Introduction   1
    Institutional Ethnography: Using Texts to Examine the
    Individual-Institutional Connection   5
    Who and Why?   7

1   The Economic and Social Context of Grocery Shopping   13
    The Household   14
    Food Experts   17
    Economic Institutions: Supermarket   20
    Supermarket Design   22
    Rise of Marketing and Advertising   25
    Consumer Sovereignty   27

2   The Work of Grocery Shopping   31
    Planning   32
    Division of Labor   37
    At the Store   40
    Conclusion   43

3   Shopping and the Nutrition Discourse   45
    Nutrition Knowledge   47
    Institutional Agents   53
    Examples of Nutrition Discourse   55
    Shopping for Nutrition   58
    Conclusion   63

4   The Efficient Housewife Discourse   65
    Efficient Housewife Discourse   69
    Notes from Real Life   74
    Conclusion   81

5   The Consumer Control Discourse   85
    Managers and Practice   86
    Advertisement Production   90

The Food Show   92
Know Your Customer   93
Build Relationships   96
Notes from Real Life   99
Conclusion   101

6   Competing Discourses and the Work of Food Shopping   105
Discourses in Contradiction   108
Social Organization of the Economy   109
Gendered Economy   110

Appendix   **113**

Bibliography   **115**

Index   **129**

Acknowledgments

I tell my students when they read a journal article or book that what they see is just the final product in a long, unrecognized, and often unrecorded process (not unlike food provisioning, actually). This project is no different and was made possible by the instruction and support of many amazing educators. My parents, Dick and LaVernne Koch, both public school teachers, instilled a love of learning from my earliest days. My mentor, advisor, dissertation chair, and friend Joey Sprague believed in this project and stood by me every step of the way. I am thankful for her guidance and her willingness to read seemingly endless drafts of this project. I was also fortunate to have Bob Antonio's support and sage advice throughout the many years of this journey. I can't thank them enough.

Along the way, faculty members Shirley Hill and Mehrengiz Najafizadeh provided guidance as mentors and committee members. The sociology department at the University of Kansas provided research and travel funding for several stages of this project. I was also lucky enough to be a member of a cohort of supportive feminist graduate students who made the slog through graduate school and the dissertation process bearable. Melissa Freiburger helped me work through methodological issues and talked food with me; without the unlimited support and reassurance from Kelley Massoni that this research was important, this book never would have happened. I am also thankful to those who cared for and educated my children as I was researching, writing, and rewriting this manuscript.

I am especially indebted to the shoppers and managers who shared their experiences with me. I want to thank Cliff in particular for his helpful assistance. The editorial staff at Berg was also central to this project; Louise Butler at Berg not only believed in this research but helped me through the transition from dissertation to manuscript. Sophie Hodgson walked me through its completion. I am most grateful to the reviewers, especially Tracey Deutsch, for their excellent comments and suggestions as well.

My spouse, Gary Foulke, a teacher and elementary school principal, never faltered in his belief in me and the importance of this project. Thank you for your love and support. My children kept me grounded and honest. Jessica, Meredith, and Haydyn, I love you and am grateful for the joy you bring to me. I wish for you a better world where caring for life is paramount.

Introduction

Food is a frequent media topic. From cable TV shows featuring expert chefs, food challenges, and extreme couponing to nightly news segments on the obesity epidemic and exposés on food production, we are a nation obsessed with food. Policy makers, journalists, and food scholars often highlight the negative consequences of our food system. According to the CDC, one-third of U.S. adults (33.8 percent) are obese and approximately 17 percent (12.5 million) children and adolescents from two to nineteen years are obese (CDC 2011). Attention to this problem has drawn high-profile politicians and celebrities into the spotlight to provide solutions to this national disorder, many of which involve parents making better choices for their families. Michelle Obama, for example, has assumed the role of anti-obesity crusader and launched a new campaign called "Let's Move: America's Move to Raise a Healthier Generation of Kids." Her advice to parents involves certain shopping and feeding changes including "eating five fruits and vegetables a day," "switching to low or non-fat milk, yogurt and cheese," drinking less soda, switching to low-sugar breakfast cereals, and leaving a bowl of fruit or carrot sticks on the kitchen table (www.letsmove.gov).

Celebrity chefs are also trying to improve our eating habits. Jamie Oliver, an internationally known chef and anti-obesity crusader, has identified the household as one of the culprits in our dysfunctional food system. In one TED (Technology, Entertainment, Design) Talks conference presentation, he looks directly at a young mother with her household's weekly food choices piled on the table: pizza, corn dogs, cheesy casseroles, and soda. Jamie Oliver peers at the table and then at this mother and says:

"I need you to know this is going to kill your children early. How does this make you feel?"

The mother tearfully replies, "I'm feeling sad and depressed. I want my kids to succeed in life . . . but I'm killing them."

Oliver's response: "Yes you are. But we can stop that" (TED Conferences 2010).

How does Oliver propose to help this woman stop killing her children? First, he would put a food ambassador in every store to teach her how to shop and how to cook convenient, healthy meals. Secondly, manufacturers and retailers would reform product labeling so she would have more information about her food choices. Third, big industry would put food education at the heart of its practice. Most importantly, she would teach her kids about food by cooking more at home, thereby helping them learn where their food comes from as well as life-long cooking skills.

Obesity is not the only food-related issue that has been featured in the mainstream media. Concerns about the production of food, especially industrial agriculture, have surfaced in literary critiques such as Eric Schlosser's *Fast Food Nation* (2001) and Michael Pollan's *The Omnivore's Dilemma* (2007), leading to the influential documentary film *Food, Inc*. These books and films focus on the problems associated with industrial agricultural production such as monocultures and pesticide use, food as a commodity, environmental effects of food, and even the treatment of farm animals.

These critiques also provide solutions for changing the agro-food system. The website from *Food, Inc.* provides ten simple things we can do to change our food system. Seven of these involve some kind of individual action such as buying organic or at farmers' markets, eating at home, or supporting laws requiring chain restaurants to post calorie information (www.foodincmovie.com).

Michael Pollan argues that in order to resist the industrial food complex we should follow one basic rule: Eat food, not too much, mostly plants (Pollan 2007). He uses our grandmothers as examples to emulate and instructs us not to eat anything they wouldn't recognize as food. Mark Bittman, a *New York Times* op-ed columnist and food critic, offers his solution to our food problems in a piece called "Food Manifesto for the Future":

> Encourage and subsidize home cooking . . . When people cook their own food, they make better choices. When families eat together, they're more stable. We should provide food education for children (a new form of home ec, anyone?), cooking classes for anyone who wants them and even cooking assistance for those unable to cook for themselves. (Bittman 2011)

On the surface, these solutions appear reasonable. Why wouldn't we want individuals to eat healthier food? Of course home-cooked meals are better than eating at McDonald's! However, there is something missing in these solutions. Not only have they been ineffective, they miss the mark because they hide the significant amount of labor involved in provisioning households, which includes the planning, administration, and shopping work necessary for preparing food at home. For instance, to whom is Bittman talking when he promotes home-cooked meals? Similarly, who does Pollan expect is preparing the "just" food? Who does Mrs. Obama charge to buy the five servings of fruits and vegetables a day? I argue that our current focus on the type of food we eat and how we are supposed to eat it renders the work of planning, shopping, and preparing the food invisible.

We don't appreciate the work involved in grocery shopping and feeding households because it is often hidden behind our belief in consumer choice. The solutions to our food problems listed above involve changes in individual behavior, specifically individuals *as consumers* making different choices at the grocery store, at the restaurant, and at the stove. These changes include eating more food (fruits and vegetables, at home, slowly) and eating less food (fats and salt, processed, fast). Implicitly, the message is that if individuals were just more disciplined or more motivated *and* they had the correct information, our families and children would not be so fat or so diseased.

In the academic food literature, there is some debate over the efficacy of an individual-level solution that would produce a significant change in our food supply as well as our bodies. On one hand, scholars consider consumers active agents who play a significant role in shaping the food system (Lockie 2002; Miller 1998; Szasz 2007; Zukin and Maguire 2004). Locavores champion small-scale farming, farmers' markets, and community-supported agriculture (all strategies that require a nonindustrial consumer model) and tout this type of shopping as a new form of activism. Related to alternative shopping, Jaffee and Gertler (2006) argue that "re-skilling" shoppers to be more aware of the food they buy could possibly force changes in the production and retail systems.

Others question the efficacy of individual-level solutions to change entrenched market patterns (DuPuis and Goodman 2005; Guthman 2004, 2007; Johnston and Szabo 2011; Roff 2007). Guthman (2004, 2008) pointedly challenges the possibility of nonmarket solutions such as individual choice as a solution to market problems and counsels for the need to reengage with the state through regulation of agriculture and food. Roff (2007) questions individual-level activism as a strategy for significant changes in the food on our shelves based on her research on genetically modified organisms (GMO) activism. Johnston and Szabo (2011) have explored consumer reflexivity at Whole

Foods Market and found the possibility of making systemic changes through organic and natural food shopping much more difficult in a corporate environment, the main goal of which is to provide pleasurable consumer choices.

While these critics analyze the politics of food, they don't often discuss the work necessary to plan, buy, and prepare food. This blind spot is a result of the complexity of studying an activity that straddles the private and public spheres, but it also occurs because consumption is taken for granted and denigrated (Zukin and Maguire 2004). Grocery shopping takes place in the space between the formal economy and the household and remains under-theorized in part because it involves unpaid labor, but mainly because most food shoppers, especially shoppers for households, are women.

Marjorie DeVault's groundbreaking work in *Feeding the Family* laid the foundation for how to approach grocery shopping as gendered market labor necessary for the larger enterprise of provisioning the household. She highlighted the important work that provisioners do to mesh what they encounter in the market with the needs of their families. She argues:

> [W]hen shoppers engage the market as context, they do enter a kind of struggle. They must deal with the superfluity of products and information about them, and with essentially antagonistic marketing techniques designed to disrupt their routines and induce them to buy new products. In this context, the screening and sorting shoppers do is a specific kind of skilled practice, but one that goes relatively unnoticed. It is essential to the operation of a market economy, but it is experienced—if noticed at all—as activity conducted primarily for the family. (DeVault 1991: 70)

Building on DeVault's research, I explore the work of provisioning in an era of neoliberal economics and politics. The "free" market has become the dominant social institution in the last twenty years, driving not only production and consumption but also the structure of the household and how we think about our relationship to each. Corporate consolidation in food manufacturing, distribution, and retail in addition to deregulation in government oversight has meant more industry control over what gets produced and what gets to the shelves (Lawrence and Burch 2007). The contraction of the state has left the household more exposed to market swings as social safety nets are removed. Consumers are left to their own devices to choose products, and mothers must rely on wages or their ability to stretch wages to make ends meet.

In addition to the labor involved in provisioning households, the context in which shoppers learn what to expect from the market and the ways in which they negotiate, evaluate, and even resist the social organization of the food system is a neglected part of the story. Institutional ethnography (described further on) is one of the few methods that allow us to explore the connection between lived experience and social structure. In other words, this method allows us to uncover the social organization of daily life starting from the standpoint of the people who actually do the daily work. Dorothy Smith, who developed institutional ethnography, argues that instead of studying society as an entity that exists outside of direct human experience, the goal of research should be to understand how our social world is put together from the standpoint of the people who are living it and use that information to uncover the social relations that shape their local experiences (Smith 1987, 1990).

INSTITUTIONAL ETHNOGRAPHY: USING TEXTS TO EXAMINE THE INDIVIDUAL-INSTITUTIONAL CONNECTION

Institutional ethnography is thus a two-step method: individuals share with the researcher a description of how they accomplish the everyday activities that sustain individuals and institutions. Using these descriptions the researcher then investigates how managers and workers in organizations coordinate and shape experience in ways shoppers often cannot see.

For example, the people who know us and our families do not make the decisions that determine the organization of our everyday lives. Instead, institutions such as corporations, governments, professional settings and organizations, universities, public schools, hospitals, and clinics determine what gets produced and how it gets distributed. Smith elaborates:

> The relations and organizations in which these individuals are active are also those that organize our lives and in which we in various ways participate. Watching television, reading the newspaper, going to the grocery store, taking a child to school, taking a mortgage out for a home, walking down a city street, switching on a light, plugging in a computer—these daily acts articulate us into social relations of the order I have called ruling as well as those of the economy; what we pick up when we are shopping will likely have been produced by people living far away from us whom we'll never know . . . The functions of "knowledge, judgment and will" have become built into a specialized complex of objectified forms of

organization and consciousness that organize and coordinate people's everyday lives. (Smith 2005: 18)

We are not often aware of these relationships because they are diffused through society and manage daily life through the use of texts (Smith 1987, 1999, 2005). Smith's conception of text includes "the association of words or images with some definite material form that is capable of replication" (Smith 2005: 166). The material forms of texts include print, film, television, audio, and electronic media, all of which have the ability to be replicated in exact form in many different places. Institutions use these texts to coordinate and standardize the work of many people in many different locales; thus, texts "coordinate the work done by different people not only in that setting but in other settings so that the work done in one place is coordinated with that done elsewhere and at other times" (Smith 2005: 166).

A good illustration of how organizations increasingly rely on more abstract methods of management is the shift in the configuration of the grocery store to supermarkets during this century. Grocery stores prior to World War II were often run by families living in the neighborhood who knew where their customers lived, how many children they had, even how they liked their meat cut. For better or worse, the connection was direct and personal. In the contemporary economy, supermarkets are both organized and managed by people who work at head-quarters many states (or even countries) away. Smith calls this new abstract form of organization "relations of ruling," which includes bureaucracy, adminis-tration, management, professional organizations, and media as well as scien-tific, technical, and cultural discourses that coordinate through the use of texts.

Texts transmit discourses that constrain or organize what people can say, think, or do. Smith's conception borrows from Foucault's understanding of discourse as regulated practices of knowledge but situates these discourses in people's everyday lives as the "local practices of translocally organized so-cial relations" (Griffith and Smith 2005). She also stresses that discourses not only regulate and control, they also provide means of action (Griffith and Smith 2005). People participate in discourse, and their participation repro-duces the social relations of production. Discourses are not determinate: people can choose to ignore these discourses in their actions and thoughts, but they are still ultimately socially accountable for the knowledge transmit-ted. Discourses are thus an important feature of contemporary life that shape people's everyday actions.

WHO AND WHY?

Grocery shopping, or the work of selecting and purchasing food for households, is the main avenue for food to enter households in the United States. Although other organizations purchase and provide food, including schools, prisons, and restaurants, the household is one of the most significant institutions for feeding individuals and families. In our contemporary society, most of the food purchased by households in the United States comes from the supermarket. It is the household shopper who is responsible for purchasing healthy and appropriate food for the family. Thus, I began my investigation into the social organization of shopping from the standpoint of shoppers who perform most of the shopping for households with dependent children. Shopping for others, especially children, is not only more challenging, but costs more; on average a household with children spends $127 more per month on food than a childless household (Food Marketing Institute 2011).

To begin to investigate the institution, I interviewed twenty grocery shoppers who shopped at three different Midwest retail locations: one regional supermarket, one large discount independent, and one rural independent. I solicited their participation through a snowball sample starting with the neighborhood school in the rural case, and through local contacts, several elementary schools, and one mothers' group in the suburban case. I also advertised for fathers' participation on the suburban town website but did not receive viable responses. The shoppers I interviewed ranged in age from twenty-four to sixty, were all white, and included one man. Although the sample was racially homogenous due to the demographics of the region, I did attempt to include a wide range of education levels, number of children, and workforce participation (see the Appendix for full demographic information). Most of the interviews lasted one to one and a half hours, with follow-ups for clarification in several cases.

The shoppers I interviewed do not constitute a sample in the traditional sense, but rather an entry point into a common set of organizational processes (DeVault and McCoy 2007) and were used to open a window into how people participate in an institutional order and how this order could be investigated (Griffith and Smith 2005). I chose different retail sites to account for different organizational settings: for example, one suburban store is independently owned, the other is part of a regional chain of stores, and the rural store is independently owned but part of a retail cooperative. Thus, the information the shoppers provided is not meant to be representative of all shoppers but provides a vantage point from the lives of those who share their experiences to investigate how their work is shaped by social relations often outside their purview.

I also interviewed the store managers about their work in organizing the retail environment. I formally interviewed the manager/owner of the rural grocery store, the head manager of the discount store, and the assistant manager of the chain store. I also informally interviewed the produce, dairy, and meat managers of the rural store while I attended a food show with them. This food exposition, discussed in more detail in Chapter 5, included over 120 vendors showing thousands of new products to store owners and managers, including Proctor and Gamble, Kraft, and Con-Agra. I also interviewed one corporate sales manager at the corporate headquarters.

Interviewing front-line workers in the institution is the first step in the institutional ethnography process. People describe their work, and from their descriptions researchers can then identify texts that participants use to help them make decisions and direct their everyday activities. In the interviews, I also inquired about the texts shoppers and managers used to help them with their work. I analyzed the texts that they consider relevant to their work, searching for themes and discourses that were identified in the interviews. These texts included women's magazines (*More*, *Good Housekeeping*, *Real Simple*), morning and evening news shows (*The Today Show*, *Good Morning America*), diet programs (i.e., Weight Watchers), government publications (i.e., United States Department of Agriculture, Health and Human Services), advertising texts, and retail trade publications (*Progressive Grocer* and *Supermarket News*).

In analyzing these texts, I searched *More*, *Good Housekeeping*, *Simple Living*, and *Weight Watchers* for articles related to shopping and nutrition published in the last four years. Articles specifically on grocery shopping were only written sporadically, but health and nutrition were topics in nearly every issue. In these cases I looked for articles that had some connection to products that one should buy for individual or household health. Large multimedia corporations own multiple publications and much of the content was repetitive.

Managers indicate that they read trade industry publications, especially *Progressive Grocer* and *Supermarket News*, general marketing newsletters printed by organizations such as the Food Marketing Institute, specific corporate newsletters, food and beverage magazines, as well as business newspapers such as *The Wall Street Journal*. I analyzed these publications for articles on consumers and consumer management.

This book attempts to link the actual experience of grocery shoppers and managers with the social organization of the food industry, which coordinates the work of grocery shopping through texts and discourses. Keep in mind that not all shoppers or managers follow what these discourses tell them to do, nor are those who make the discourses trying to control the minds of grocery shoppers. The power of institutional ethnography is that it allows us to step into the flow of organizational relationships at a certain time and place to "see" social forces that shape (but do not necessarily determine) our activities in ways that are often invisible to us.

After summarizing the work of shopping as described by the individuals in my study, I discuss three discourses that shape the work of grocery shopping in the twenty-first century in the United States. These may not be the only discourses that shape provisioning, but were the most salient for the shoppers I interviewed. The first discourse, which I call the "efficient housewife," advises consumers to be rational and efficient with their time and money and offers strategies such as clipping coupons, shopping the sales, even shopping on a full stomach to avoid unnecessary purchases. While this sounds reasonable, the actual work involved in being efficient is quite complicated and labor intensive. Many shoppers used strategies presented by this discourse, especially those who were on a tight budget or described themselves as cost-conscious, but others had the option of disregarding these messages because they could afford to.

A second discourse, "individual responsibility for nutrition," is a science-based consumer education model that reduces food to parts such as carbohydrates and fats and makes reading the label more important than taste or quality in choosing food. This discourse not only obscures more qualitative aspects of food but makes the individual responsible for choosing healthy food in a world of prepared dinners and cheap junk food. Almost all shoppers referenced this discourse, but those who were attuned to this discourse, especially professional and middle-class shoppers, expressed more anxiety about following (or not being able to follow) the messages of this discourse.

The third discourse that influenced shoppers is the "consumer control" discourse, which was expressed by managers and found in industry publications. This discourse extols the customer as "queen," but actively works to manage and control what and how consumers buy. Not only do marketers instruct managers to accumulate data on consumers in order to shape what they buy, marketers also suggest strategies to shape the retail environment in ways that distract and psychologically disrupt the shoppers in order to increase their purchases.

Instead of helping shoppers make good food choices, these discourses are often in contradiction and make the work of shopping more difficult. The "efficiency discourse" that teaches shoppers to be efficient with time and money often precludes buying healthier, more expensive food as instructed by the nutrition discourse. The "consumer control" discourse contradicts the other two by providing managers and store owners with strategies to encourage impulse buying. In addition to making shopping more difficult and labor intensive, these discourses assume an abstract consumer making autonomous decisions rather than individuals trying to feed families and direct them to shop in ways that do not necessarily make their lives easier. In other words, discourses assume a standardized consumer and in the process obscure the real-life situations of food provisioners. Are you short on money to pay for groceries? Cut more coupons. Don't have time to make dinner every night because you work two jobs? Spend more time planning. Have a picky child? Make several healthy meals.

By illuminating these discourses we uncover a specific social organization of the food system that depends on women's unpaid labor in the home and at the grocery store but renders this work invisible and more challenging because of these inconsistent messages. We will see that shoppers can disregard the discourses, and do resist in ways that make sense to them given their social position and the material constraints they face. Does this mean that shoppers don't share in the responsibility to care for their households? Absolutely not. But these discourses assume the labor of the shopper, and coupled with an economic ideology that extols the supposed power of the consumer, the choices shoppers make are then equated with what they want and/or need. The system that organizes and depends on this labor is now obscured.

I argue that by looking at the social organization of shopping from the standpoint of the shopper, we find many forces that impinge on individual decision making. Consumer sovereignty, the belief that the consumer has the ultimate power in a free market society and a hallmark of neoliberalism, is not only an illusion but benefits other institutions, especially government and industry, by placing responsibility back onto consumers for their choices. Making good choices is not nearly as easy as it sounds, but it is more convenient for government agencies and the food industry to individualize these problems than to provide systemic changes. I argue in the last chapter that more consumer knowledge and education (our current policy direction) will not be successful without concomitant changes in retail strategies, government policies, and economic programs that support provisioning over profit. This research suggests that individual changes are necessary but not sufficient for social change; without recognizing to what extent institutions shape our decisions, we cannot fully affect systemic changes.

It is my hope that by exploring the social organization of grocery shopping, we can break down the illusion that individual purchasing is the only way to make social change and begin to find ways as consumers, but more importantly as citizens, to work collectively on solving issues such as food insecurity and hunger, obesity, and other health-related issues in an equitable and humane way.

–1–

The Economic and Social Context of Grocery Shopping

When an American mother buys baby carrots and a rotisserie chicken at the grocery store on her way home from work, she crosses many disciplinary boundaries. To understand the whole process, at the very least we must discuss the emotional, unpaid, and waged labor she engages in; the economics of the retail store, the producers and distributors; the policies that have shaped transportation, agriculture, and welfare; and the experts who provide her with information about food consumption. The shopper herself has a story: how she feels about feeding her family, what difficulties she encounters at the grocery store and at home, her relationships with the people she shops with and for. Thus, the oft-denigrated act of grocery shopping is a useful prism through which to view the intersection of individual choice, cultural production, and the larger political economy.

While this task appears daunting, feminist scholars have already noted that the activity of grocery shopping sits at the nexus of two vital institutions: the household and the market economy (DeVault 1991; Weinbaum and Bridges 1976). In order to ground the experiences of the shoppers presented in the following chapters, it is necessary to highlight important developments in both institutions over the course of the twentieth century. This chapter will discuss how grocery shopping has evolved with changes in household composition and the expectations of mothers, the evolution of the supermarket as a retail strategy, and the rise of food experts and marketers, all playing against the backdrop of the larger economic ethos of consumer sovereignty.

This short history will provide the scaffolding from which we can understand the discourses that shape grocery shopping, how and by whom these discourses are produced, and how these processes affect shoppers' decisions at the grocery store.

THE HOUSEHOLD

Who is doing the grocery shopping for the household? Although men have increased their share of household labor since the 1960s (Allen and Sachs 2007; Coltrane 1997; Sayer 2005), grocery shopping and food preparation are still women's work, with at least 65 percent of all grocery shopping and 68 percent of meal preparation for households done by women (U.S. Department of Labor 2007a). Marketing data suggests that shoppers with the most difficult and time-consuming work of feeding the household are shoppers with children (Coca-Cola Retailing Research Council of North America 2008). According to the American Time Use Survey, between 2003 and 2007 mothers on average spent one hour grocery shopping a week, compared to half an hour for men (U.S. Bureau of Labor Statistics 2008). However, married mothers, both fully employed and unemployed, are twice as likely to grocery shop on an average day than married fathers, employed and unemployed (U.S. Bureau of Labor Statistics 2008).

Changes over the past thirty years in women's wage labor have greatly impacted their unpaid household labor. Women, especially mothers, have entered the labor force in large numbers since the 1960s. According to the U.S. Department of Labor, women comprised 46 percent of the total U.S. labor force in 2002 and are projected to account for 47 percent of the labor force in 2016. A record 68 million women were employed in the United States—seventy-five percent of employed women worked in full-time jobs, while 25 percent worked on a part-time basis (U.S. Department of Labor 2007b). Nearly 72 percent of mothers with children under eighteen were in the labor force in 2009 (U.S. Department of Labor 2010). By contrast, in 1950, only a third of women over the age of sixteen were in the labor force (U.S. Department of Labor 2000). However, having additional children decreased mothers' paid work hours such that employment rates for mothers with four or more children was 56 percent (Krantz-Kent 2009).

In addition to being in the workforce, more women are heading households by themselves. In 2007, 23 percent of households were headed by a single mother compared to 6 percent in 1970 (Bianchi 2010). Working mothers report fewer hours devoted to housework but, with paid and unpaid labor, report higher workloads than unemployed women, often forgoing leisure and sleep to get everything done (Bianchi et al. 2000; Bianchi 2009). Eating food in restaurants is one strategy for managing this labor. In 1970, 69 percent of food was eaten at home, whereas in 2009 this figure had dropped to 51 percent (U.S. Department of Agriculture/ERS 2009). However, due to the recession grocery stores are reporting that many shoppers are going back to preparing food at home (Food Marketing Institute 2010).

One option for affluent mothers to bridge the gap between wage work and unpaid household labor is to hire domestic workers and nannies. The women now feeding some affluent families are often poor, immigrants, and/or women of color (Ehrenreich and Hochschild 2002; Tronto 2002). In addition to feeding households, women of color and immigrants are also cooking and serving our food in restaurants and schools (Liu and Apollon 2011).

Not only are women procuring and preparing food, this work is intimately connected with women's role and their identity as mothers in households. This was one of DeVault's (1991) central findings, in which she argued that food work as part of women's caring work in the household contributes to their subordination. Dorothy Smith (1999) further argues that this role of mothers as the key to healthy and successful children is central to the "standard North American family," the paradigmatic form of family that assumes a mother who subordinates her unpaid labor and attention to the needs of her children and household. In the standard North American family paradigm, mothers are primarily responsible for raising well-adjusted, healthy, and successful children regardless of the practical or material conditions in which they find themselves. Of course the reality of the family form has diverged significantly from the traditional nuclear family, but nostalgia and the social organization of society perpetuate this ideology.

"Intensive mothering" is an extension of this standard North American family ideology. Sharon Hays (1996) argues that, with the exodus of women out of the household and into the workforce, anxiety over who will provide the nurturing necessary for raising children has manifested into an all-encompassing belief in intensive motherhood. Child rearing should be child-centered, expert-guided, labor-intensive, and emotionally involved, which puts the responsibility for all facets of children's lives squarely on the shoulders of individual mothers (Hays 1996). Intensive mothering ratchets up the expectations for motherhood as a means to show our commitment to nurturing; thus, raising children is not something mothers should do on the fly without much thought and preparation, nor should mothers look to earlier generations to find examples. Food, as it connects to health, well-being, and ultimately life, is a critical responsibility of mothers and the stakes are high.

The initial choice of whether to breastfeed or use formula is a good example of the emotional and often public battle with feeding a mother faces. New mothers are often sent home with conflicting messages: breastfeeding is best, but here's a formula sample in your free diaper bag. Make sure to choose wisely. The story one mother in my study relayed about her dilemma with breastfeeding illustrates the interconnection of intensive mothering and food work. Kelly Jones had a job that she liked, but decided to stay home after she had her first child because she wasn't convinced her daughter would be fed properly without her. She says:

> And I think that the nursing thing is really more than anything, how I ended up staying home. Now looking back on it, it seems kind of silly to me but at the time, when you are that new mother and a couple months went by and your baby still wasn't taking a bottle, I just couldn't in my head figure out how she was going to eat while I wasn't there. Now if another mother would talk to me about it I would probably be able to tell her rationally, it will work out, it will be a couple week adjustment but you will figure it out. But at the time I couldn't figure it out, I felt kind of panicked about it. It wasn't worth it to me and again I was in a situation where I could make that choice with Jerry's [her husband] help but everyone can't choose to do it.

She confesses that although she enjoys staying at home with her kids, she is scared of trying to get back into the job market after a long hiatus.

The combination of intensive mothering and the new food movements (i.e., local, organic and natural foods, slow food) have silently increased expectations for feeding families. The slow food movement promotes home-cooked meals eaten in a leisurely manner to create a space in which food and sociability can be appreciated. However, eating at home with family members has diminished in large measure *because of* the increased pressure on women's time from wage work, child-related obligations, and the lack of support from spouses (Allen and Sachs 2007). Home gardening is another example of how the food movement is in contradiction with women's roles as mothers and workers. To produce food at home, women often have the triple responsibility of working, preparing dinner, and weeding the garden (or cajoling family members to do it). A frank discussion of a more gender equitable division of household labor might mitigate some of these contradictions, but doesn't appear as an important aspect of new food movements.

FOOD EXPERTS

Even though more mothers work outside the home, they are still expected to fulfill their responsibility of producing healthy and well-adjusted children. One way they are to accomplish this task is to utilize information from experts on successful child development and efficient household management. Expert knowledge about food and household management comes from dieticians, extension workers, physicians, policy makers, industry representatives, and the media sources through which this information is disseminated.

As mothers' status shifted from producer of food to consumer during the early twentieth century, their work became increasingly subject to new sources of knowledge about how to choose the right food products and produce the most efficient household. Women became food purchasers rather than growers, and as the number of choices rose at the supermarket, they needed information on how and what to purchase. While the food industry developed new marketing practices as a means to direct purchases, home economists provided information on the basics of maintaining households in a consumer society. These institutional experts stepped in to provide information on how to be a good household consumer. Using the language of science to create a more rationalized consumption system, home economists became mediators between industry, government, and consumers and played an important role in shaping consumer products and their usage (Goldstein 2006). Women and mothers did not "ingest" this information entirely or uncritically, but expert information certainly became an important point of reference for grocery shoppers in the twentieth century.

Ironically, home economics developed as an academic and practical discipline because many educated women, shut out of mainstream professions like economics, carved out a niche in the academy through domestic sciences. Ellen Richards, one of the founders of the American Home Economics

Association, was the first woman to receive a degree from MIT in chemistry. Turned down for private chemistry positions, she eventually became an instructor in "sanitary chemistry" and applied science to everyday problems women faced in their households (Stage 1997). Rather than confining women to the home but without directly challenging the cult of domesticity, Richards envisioned a place for women in the larger community based on their domestic skills. She was the chief nutritionist for the New England Kitchen in 1890, a community-based food kitchen that sold soups, stews, and puddings to the working classes to be taken home for dinner, as well as one of the founders of the Boston School of Housekeeping, which certified women in domestic service (Stage 1997).

But the larger economic ethos of the time was caught up in the efficiency movement. Frederick Taylor was developing scientific management techniques to rationalize the factory, and the home economics movement imported that shift into the household. The household became the site of women's labor and home management experts used methods taken from time and motion studies in industry to streamline household tasks such as food preparation, dishwashing, and laundry (Strasser 1982).

Christine Frederick, an early advocate of Taylor's efficiency studies and a home engineer, declared that housewives must become purchasing agents for the household: "[E]very woman running the business of homemaking must train herself to become an efficient 'purchasing agent' for her particular family or firm by study, watchfulness and practice" (Strasser 1982: 247). Scheduling and planning were crucial to efficient household management: meals should be planned one or two weeks in advance with every ingredient needed on a "purchasing sheet" (the forerunner to our modern list). Planning would keep material and financial waste down and reduce the effort expended on food preparation. For example, one type of cooking should be used in every meal to economize on effort, whether it be boiled, baked, or fried, and any food left should be incorporated into future meals. In this way, the "left over" becomes a "planned over" and waste is minimized (Strasser 1982: 214). But the overall goal of household efficiency was to save time for other household tasks such as helping the husband with his business or working with the kids.

Not only were experts rationalizing food procurement, scientists and experts were also standardizing how we should eat. Scientists working in the progressive era of the early 1900s sought changes to standardize the

American diet in the face of increasing numbers of immigrants (Levenstein 2003). Between 1880 and 1930, W. O. Atwater, a chemist and the first director of the USDA's Office of Experiment Stations, discovered that food can be broken down into constituent parts; that is, proteins, carbohydrates, and fats (Roth 2000). Dubbed the "father of American nutrition," Atwater viewed the body as a machine and food as fuel for that machine (Mudry 2006). From this mechanistic perspective, chemists and scientists who worked for the United States Department of Agriculture reduced food to its component categories—calories, fat, protein, and carbohydrates. Home economists with the USDA borrowed this scientific understanding of food to create food buying guides as early as 1917 and taught the public about proper eating using numbers (Mudry 2009).

Atwater directed his prescriptions to eat more protein to the working classes, but it was actually middle-class housewives who began to learn the vocabulary of protein, fat, and carbohydrates (Levenstein 2003). Trained home economists in the 1940s and 1950s used this foundation of efficiency and standardization to educate the public about food and household management. Home economists at this time were usually well-educated women who were writing and teaching other women to become good household managers. These women sought to educate the public through courses taught in schools, colleges, and extension services and through articles in popular publications. As more women entered the paid workforce, less time was available for housework, so these experts provided information on how to manage time effectively. Also, as new consumer products such as dishwashers and washing machines came on the market, these educators were available to advise consumers on selection and use of these new items (Stage 1997).

Although home economics went through a decline in the 1970s and 1980s, the content is still taught under the rubric of family and consumer science. The College of Home Economics at Kansas State University, for example, has been renamed the College of Human Ecology and those who complete the B.S. in human ecology are employed as educators in high schools and middle schools, as family and consumer science agents, or by 4-H youth programs with the Cooperative Extension Service (Karen Pence, Assistant Dean of College of Human Ecology, personal communication). Programs in dietetics, nutrition, public health, family studies, and human services are available at these institutions (usually land grant) and many students studying in these majors go on to work as registered dieticians and nutritionists. The Bureau of

Labor Statistics data indicate that the professions of dieticians and nutritionists are overwhelmingly female (U.S. Bureau of Labor Statistics 2009).

In addition to the professions listed above, women hold more than 60 percent of the food preparation and service jobs in the United States, often the least flexible and least remunerated jobs in the food sector (U.S. Bureau of Labor Statistics 2009). But women also account for less than 12 percent of corporate officer positions in food production, food wholesaling, and food and drug retailing (McTaggart 2005) and only 20 percent of management positions in the U.S. Department of Agriculture (U.S. Office of Personnel Management 1992). The historical trajectory of female nutritionists and educators managed by men directing female consumers continues into the twenty-first century.

This expert information is disseminated through various channels: the mainstream media, nutritionists, USDA publications, doctors' offices, and now even at supermarkets where dieticians are employed to answer consumers' questions. With this short history as a background, the intersection of food choice and nutrition in contemporary society is discussed in Chapter 3, and current advice on how to save money and manage the household efficiently is found in Chapter 4.

ECONOMIC INSTITUTIONS: SUPERMARKET

Not only do mothers encounter expert knowledge and ideologies in their role as food provider for the household, they also must navigate the grocery store with its own particular history and social organization. Most food today is purchased in supermarkets. Consumers in the United States spent nearly $557 billion on food in supermarkets in 2009 (Food Marketing Institute 2009), although alternatives to the supermarket are increasing in number and popularity, especially farmers' markets and community-supported agriculture. By contrast, sales at farmers' markets in 2006 were $1 billion, less than one percent of total food sales.

The official definition of a supermarket is "an establishment primarily engaged in retailing a general line of food, such as canned and frozen foods; fresh fruits and vegetables; and fresh and prepared meats, fish, and poultry represented as major departments, with at least $2 million in annual sales" (Kaufman 2002). This type of store, which includes stores in chains like Kroger, Publix, Safeway, and Whole Foods as well as large independently owned stores, accounted for about 60 percent of total food sales in 2010 (Food Marketing Institute 2010). Sales at supercenters (defined by the Census Bureau as "retail establishments primarily engaged in retailing a general line of groceries in combination with general lines of new merchandise, such as apparel, furniture, and appliances") are increasing as well (U.S. Department of Agriculture 2010a), especially Walmart, Costco, and Sam's Club.

Supermarkets and supercenters have assumed a more powerful position in the food industry for several reasons. First, when the U.S. government relaxed antitrust laws in the 1980s that had prevented major national and global firms from forming, corporations were allowed to expand beyond their region, which gave rise to nationally and globally oriented supermarkets (Marsden and Wrigley 2001). Second, the management model used by Walmart, which incorporated new technology and information systems, streamlined the distribution process by providing shippers with up-to-the-minute information on stock levels and devolving responsibility to them to ship the products in time to keep products on the shelves uninterrupted (Konefal et al. 2007). As more and more retailers must emulate this model to stay competitive, these administrative and technological changes have increased the power of retailers at the expense of manufacturers and the state.

Today, economic concentration, the increasing use of fast food and restaurant outlets for meals, and the entry of Walmart into the retail food market has increased the competition for supermarkets, leading to continued retail consolidation and concentration (Lawrence and Burch 2007). The top five companies in the United States—Walmart, Kroger, Albertson's, Inc., Safeway, and Ahold—account for nearly 50 percent of the grocery market (Konefal et al. 2007). Dixon (2007) argues that supermarkets have capitalized on these trends by positioning themselves as food authorities that can significantly shape the choices and lifestyles of their consumers. Large supermarket chains are now often in a position to determine what is produced, to what standards it is held, and where it is sold (Lawrence and Burch 2007).

This trajectory has also created a bifurcated market with upscale, high-quality food retailers like Whole Foods on one hand and low-price warehouse stores like Walmart on the other (McMichael and Friedmann 2007). Market-driven food retailing has also left out some shoppers, especially those in declining rural or low-income neighborhoods, creating food deserts where provisioning households is an even greater challenge.

SUPERMARKET DESIGN

While dominant today, the supermarket form took most of the last century to develop. Prior to World War II, women in rural areas often grew some of their food, supplementing it with bulk purchasing and buying canned and packaged goods at small independent grocery stores. Urban women had open markets, small neighborhood stores, consumer cooperatives, and even peddlers who provided items on horse-drawn carts (Deutsch 2010). For some urban shoppers, supermarket-type stores became increasingly available during this time.

Some of the first chain stores to develop were A&P (The Great Atlantic and Pacific Tea Company), Kroger, and Piggly Wiggly in Memphis, Tennessee. Clarence Saunders, the owner of Piggly Wiggly, introduced in 1915 the first self-service grocery store in which the customer could select her own merchandise from display counters and pay cash (Bowlby 1997; Humphery 1998; Zimmerman 1955). This store also featured the first checkout stands, prices marked on all products, and a full line of nationally advertised brands. By 1960, supermarkets sold nearly 70 percent of all of America's food (Humphery 1998). The supermarket expanded rapidly due to a growing postwar economic prosperity, increasing suburbanization, and the widespread use and ownership of the automobile. In the last twenty years, the supermarket strategy has extended in both directions—to larger hypermarket-type stores on one end down to convenience stores with a small assortment of grocery items at higher cost on the other. Today, the average American supermarket measures over forty-six thousand square feet and displays over 48,750 items (Food Marketing Institute 2009).

The design and organizational strategy of the supermarket also differed from previous retail models. Independent mom and pop stores stocked few products, marked prices high but expected to sell fewer products, had limited advertising, and, most significantly for customers, did not require them to physically choose the products themselves. Clerks, often the store owner or a family member, would measure products from the bulk bin or retrieve the product from the shelf at the behest of the customer.

One of the stores in my study began as a small mom and pop store at the turn of the century. Charles O'Donnell, the father of the current owner I interviewed for this study, worked in his family's store in the 1930s and 1940s. The store Charles' father owned and managed measured roughly 700 square feet and provided staples like bread, bulk flour and beans, and an assortment of brand-name canned goods. In this town where Charles lived and worked, six small stores sold food to a population of about 1,000. None of the stores had more than four or five workers, and most were family owned and run. The farmers' cooperative was the biggest store with two paid employees.

According to Charles, grocery shopping was a relatively uncomplicated affair:

Shoppers didn't have any grocery buggies to put them in. They would bring the list of what they wanted and they would tell you and you would fill their order and put it on the counter right there and they paid for it and boxed it up. If they had more than they could carry we would carry it out for them but usually they would carry their own groceries out. Behind the counter there was tall shelving with canned goods on it and you had a grabber and you could take any can off that you wanted. And some of them had a rolling ladder that you could crawl up the ladder and get it off, you know. But they put the order up and they would pay for it right there and take it out. They would wait while you got their order ready.

Family labor made these stores viable. Charles' father worked with his wife and two children for many years, eventually hiring one extra employee later on. When Charles took over the store in the 1950s, he worked with his wife and children in the same manner. The hours were long: set hours from eight to six and then several hours of inventory after closing. He remembers being somewhat irritated when his customers would leave their grocery order with him on Saturday nights and come back, sometimes as late as midnight, after watching the weekly movie in the theater down the street.

When asked to characterize the difference between shopping then and now, he recalled that the store owners knew each customer personally as well as their children's names and what family they came from. People shopped in the same store because they had credit at the store, and many farm families

Figure 1.1   Picture of O'Donnell's grocery store from the 1930s.

would only pay once a year. Much of the food sold was locally or regionally produced, arriving usually by train or truck from the larger town twenty miles away. The store family and the seasonal employees it hired did a significant part of the work of shopping by filling people's orders and delivering groceries to those who lived outside of town as well as shut-ins. Shopping was integrated into the life of the community.

But mom and pop stores and open markets were not without issues for shoppers. In some small independent stores, managers did not mark prices on the items, so bargaining and haggling was common. Some owners charged their richer customers more but also had difficulty collecting from some of them (Greer 1986). Tracey Deutsch (2002, 2010) provides a well-documented account of the tensions inherent in shopping, particularly at urban stores, at the turn of the century. In stores shoppers often found their purchases controlled and scrutinized by male shop clerks and owners in which "every transaction meant implicit and explicit statements of women's fitness as wives, mothers, shoppers and homemakers" (Deutsch 2002: 157). Ethnic tensions arose in larger cities as African Americans and immigrants faced discrimination in white-owned grocery stores. Deutsch (2010) argues these racialized and gendered relationships contributed to the rise of chains stores, especially in larger urban areas.

Self-service, one significant aspect of the new supermarket design, mitigated some of the personal tension between shoppers and owners but also set the stage for the rise of a new consumption-based society. Products now became the focus of retailing, and as food prices began to drop through the efficiencies created by an industrially based agriculture, more attention and money were devoted to promoting these products through marketing and advertising. One new supermarket strategy involved rearranging the store to put the product and the consumer in immediate contact with each other. One retailing strategist in 1935 stated: "As far as possible every square inch of the eyes' range of vision, from the top of the shelving down to the floor, wherever the customer stands, wherever she looks, should display merchandise" (Dipman quoted in Bowlby 1997). The counter was eliminated and the shelves were low enough that the customer could reach for any item she wanted. Customer movement also had to be regulated to maximize purchases; hence the paradigmatic placement of the dairy section at the back of the store to ensure the customer would have to walk by many different products to get the one item she really needed. By 1953, self-service had become the norm: over 90 percent of all supermarkets had complete self-service dairy departments, and prepackaged produce departments were found in 44 percent (Mayo 1993).

RISE OF MARKETING AND ADVERTISING

For the grocery store, not only did self-service decrease labor costs, it also encouraged an unprecedented rise in impulse (or unplanned) purchases. Market research indicated that between 1949 and 1965 almost three-fourths of all supermarket food purchases were unplanned (Levenstein 2003), and today industry analysts estimate that at least one-half to two-thirds of purchases are a result of impulse buying (Underhill 1999). During the early period of the supermarket, established manufacturers were alarmed by this trend because it allowed new products to be directly chosen by customers without the intervention of a clerk, but it soon became clear this could actually benefit manufacturers. One industrial designer wrote: "In the modern supermarket women are no longer cajoled into buying a particular brand. As a result, an entirely new kind of package design has developed . . . the ladies who trundle their little shopping wagons among the shelves and tables need packaging to entice them to read products" (Egmont Arens 1950, quoted in Levenstein 2003). Paul Willis, an early president of the Grocery Manufacturers of America, emphasized the importance of marketing:

> When grocers had store clerks, they could influence what consumers purchased. By eliminating the store clerks, self-service gave consumers an uninterrupted opportunity to make their own choice. By displaying the manufacturers' products instead of hiding them behind the counter, supermarkets gave branded products an opportunity to be chosen. (Willis quoted in Greer 1986)

Marketing developed as a way to shape the relationship between the product and the customer. A contemporary introductory marketing text defines the goal of marketing as satisfying consumers: "Successful marketing is customer driven: it addresses customer needs and desires" (Churchill and Peter 1995). But as marketing became an integral aspect of the supermarket model, marketing strategists focused less on selling specific products and more on influencing the consumer to make a purchase (Dawson 2003). The Grocery Manufacturers of America currently defines shopper marketing solely in terms of influencing the shopper to make a purchase and includes "all marketing stimuli, developed based on a deep understanding of shopper behavior, attitudes and emotions, designed to build brand equity, designed to engage the shopper (i.e. consumer in 'shopping mode') and lead him/her to make a purchase" (Grocery Manufacturers of America 2008).

Marketing strategies include singling out individual customers, often as a "type" based on demographic information and shopping patterns, and altering the shopping environment to get customers to accept new products or to increase the number of products included in the shopping cart (Dawson 2003: 52). Manufacturers now spend billions of dollars to insert themselves between the consumer and the product; in 2000, for example, marketing expenditures by food companies, which included advertising and discount incentives like coupons and slotting fees, totaled $33 billion (Nestle 2002). Seventy percent of the total advertising bill was spent marketing convenience foods, whereas 2.2 percent went to promote fruits, vegetables, grains, and beans (which constitute the bulk of acceptable foods on the food pyramid). Marketing is thus about managing the customer before, during, and after the shopping event.

CONSUMER SOVEREIGNTY

As self-service placed consumers in direct contact with the products and as consumption in general became the basis for economic growth, it was an easy leap to elevate the "market" (that nebulous place where abstract buyers and sellers come together to make each other happy) as a key institution in our national prosperity. In terms of food consumption, the market has supposedly given consumers the power to make choices about their own and their family's well-being. Implicit in the debate about how and what we should eat is the ideology of consumer sovereignty that pervades this mainstream economic thinking. Consumer sovereignty is a belief derived from neoclassical economics that individuals are merely rational choice makers who decide what to buy without much interference from outside sources (in other words, their choices are exogenous). If a shopper decides to buy X product, it is because he or she has determined it is in his or her best interest (it will increase their utility) to choose that product. Consumer sovereignty doesn't leave room to account for outside influences such as advertising, a child whining, or experts who advise us, all of which influence what and how we buy.

Consumer sovereignty is one of the core beliefs of the consumer society. Thomas Princen (2005: 150) summarizes the logic of consumer sovereignty:

> [P]roducers respond to consumer demand by producing the goods the consumer wants and at a price the consumer will pay. If the consumer doesn't buy the product, producers don't make it. Governments do likewise; they intervene in the economy to serve the consumer . . . [S]overeign consumers are entitled to have their desires satisfied, to have ever more goods, and to do so all at low, low prices.

The consumer sovereignty discourse emphasizes that individuals know best what they want to buy, and there should be no interference between the consumers and their products from markets or governments.

Ultimately, consumer sovereignty supposedly reflects a kind of economic democracy: consumers vote with their dollar, making "choices" about what products should make it into their homes and what shouldn't. The consumer sovereignty discourse doesn't discriminate or rank between choices; the larger test of these choices is whether they increase the Gross Domestic Product (GDP) (Galbraith 2004). The market doesn't discriminate between Coke or bottled water, so long as consumers are still buying products. If consumers are buying Coke, for example, that must be what they really want.

The Food Marketing Institute, one of the largest and most influential organizations promoting information and programs for retailers and wholesalers in the United States, provides the basic message of the consumer sovereignty discourse in one of its newsletters: "The singular force driving the [food] revolution is the consumer. The consumer's market power is growing strong and ingrained" (Food Marketing Institute 2005). Royalty is not even an accurate description of the consumers' role: "An old industry truism holds that 'the consumer is king.' Food retailers today would update that saying to 'the consumer is dictator'" (Food Marketing Institute 2007). Another industry publication claims the consumer's power is due to economic law: "Consumers come out ahead, because the laws of supply, demand and competition almost always favor the customer" (Janoff 2000: 36).

This discourse seeps into popular media:

> In the end, there are a couple things these die-hard competitors all seem to agree on. In a country where so many people are looking for such different things, the mass in mass marketing is probably a thing of the past. And who wins from all that competition? The consumer of course. (Alfano 2005)

In a neoliberal economic era, shopping has supposedly become an experience in which powerful consumers get their needs met through their purchases. The shopper is now queen and her choices reign supreme. But the responsibility for making good choices is also all her own. The ideology of consumer sovereignty hides the work of organizations in producing, manufacturing, and retailing the products people buy; how experts shape how we think about food and shopping; how products and shopping get promoted; and especially the work that individuals do at all stages of the consumption process. This ideology also disregards the structural factors that influence what people can buy, including income, access to stores, and manufacturers' agreements with distributors, among others. For household shoppers, the combination of complete self-service in an economically asymmetrical retail environment and an increased focus on the responsibility of mothers to choose the right food for their children makes them doubly responsible for what happens in their households, both as consumers and as mothers. In the next chapter, I will explore how shoppers describe the experience of food provisioning, including the work involved, how they feel about this work, and what textual sources they use to make decisions at the grocery store.

–2–

The Work of Grocery Shopping

As little research has been done from the perspective of grocery shoppers, I was interested in how shoppers felt about this activity. More than half of the shoppers in my study expressed some level of enjoyment in shopping: it got them out of the house, they saw people they knew, or they simply enjoyed the act of choosing products. Karen Calhoun told me she liked to shop, especially as she was no longer working and could go during the day when the stores were less crowded. Maggie Waggoner said, "I very much enjoy grocery shopping. It puts me in a different place mentally and for me I see it as relaxing and I see it as an opportunity to get out of the house."

Conversely, some shoppers were explicit in their distaste for grocery shopping. Jessica Pierce said, "I don't like grocery shopping. We are always in a hurry. For a grocery store trip if I can get in and out in fifteen minutes I'm really happy." But almost all of the shoppers I talked to agreed with Jackie Engle in some way: "Grocery shopping is just something I have to do."

That grocery shopping is still part of women's household work is evident from the statistics presented in the previous chapter, but what does this work entail? Marjorie DeVault (1991) studied the work of grocery shopping in her classic book, *Feeding the Family*. She found that grocery shopping is more than a simple matter of buying a few things that one needs, because "needs" grow out of a routine that develops over time and what is bought at the store is often an extension of the work of maintaining family relationships. The grocery routine is based on what family members like to eat or must eat, family schedules, and household financial constraints; in other words, "deci-sions are linked to the resources and characteristics of particular households and features of the market" (DeVault 1991: 71). In this chapter, we will hear about shoppers' experiences with provisioning their households and from their descriptions we can then begin to uncover the social organization that coordinates this work. All names used in the book are pseudonyms.

PLANNING

Shoppers do not go into the store and pick out food randomly. The shop-ping trip is the tip of the iceberg in terms of the work involved in feeding families. Food provisioning generally involves a planning phase, which in-cludes making meal plans, knowing what meals and foods the household members can or will eat, and scheduling meals and shopping trips around the activities of household members. While studies from the 1980s and 1990s found that food providers often deferred to their husbands' wants and needs (Charles and Kerr 1988; Murcott 1983), recent studies find that now children's needs are just as salient. Dixon argues that "children are as potent a boundary setter for what food comes into the house as is defer-ence to men" (Dixon 1999: 63).

Shoppers engage in different levels of planning. For some, planning for the shopping trip may be as elaborate as sitting down on Sunday night to plan out the entire week's menu, or it may be as hasty as jotting a few items down on a sticky note to pick up that night after work. But even for the provisioners who don't spend much time on meal planning, managing schedules and tak-ing into account when people will be able to eat and when they can get to the store is a significant task.

Jane Smith, a part-time worker with six kids, regularly makes meal menus to save money on eating out but also tries to include her kids in this planning. She said:

> I let the kids pick once a week. They get to pick their own dinner menu and the only rule is no macaroni and cheese and no hot dogs. I usually buy the things they pick for the week. I make a week menu or otherwise I go "what am I gonna cook?" and I don't have the things I need to cook and we don't eat or we order pizza and we can't afford to eat out. So we try to make a menu and stick to that menu . . . I just tried a new recipe last night. It wasn't very good. Jerry liked it, the kids hated

it. It was an enchilada casserole. Jerry and I thought it was really good but the kids were like "Mom, this is gross." So I don't think I'll make it again.

Jane also has to consider health issues when planning her food lists:

We use frozen vegetables because Marney has kidney stones and she can't have all that salt from canned vegetables. Unless the canned vegetables are on a really good sale, it is mostly frozen.

Some mothers in my study had different planning issues. Rather than planning for the week, the meal menu or item list was often done at work or in the store or the menu problem was perhaps solved by eating out. I usually began the interviews by asking shoppers to remember the last time they went to the grocery store. Jessica Pierce, a full-time worker and mother of two, pulled out her Blackberry, tried to recall the last time she went shopping based on the "other events in my life at that moment in time," and then elaborated:

Shopping is not on the schedule so it just happens when it happens so I have to put it in terms of what else happens that day . . . Let's see, it was after work, I just had to figure out which day after work. Because I don't schedule it, it happens when I think that maybe there are some things that need to happen at home. So it's not like I plan a menu and go and grab things, it's more like "is there something at home? No, probably not" so I probably ought to get something that could possibly turn into a meal that evening. [Do you plan for several meals?] I would probably try to plan for a couple of meals but sometimes it's a daily just go to the store grab and grab something for that evening. I'm there a lot, probably more than if I would plan a menu and carry through, but I don't do that.

While Jessica doesn't necessarily have time to plan meals, another reason she shops regularly is that her son is very particular about the food he eats. She said:

Evan [her son] has a bit of a regurgitation issue. At will. And if today he wants broccoli, he'll eat broccoli, but if he wanted green beans and I served broccoli, he can regurgitate his whole meal in about one second. Because that's not what he wanted . . . So partially you have to shop daily to get his choices.

Maggie Waggoner's shopping and planning have changed in large part because she has switched jobs. She said:

> I used to be a meal planner. I used to have a weekly menu written out so everybody could look and know what we were having every day and it was all written out and I would shop for that menu when I was in town. And I would say in the last two years since my job changed last year, I have gotten away from that planning and shopping once a week. [Because of the change in your job?] I think so. I think part of it, especially this year, is the hours I put in. I am putting in so much time, through most of the winter I wouldn't even leave work until six. So it was just kind of like, I'd go home, you know, it was like, what do I have on hand? What can I quick stop and get? I wasn't near as organized about it.

While time is one important factor in how she shops, family members' likes and dislikes are also a part of how she considers what to make:

> Tim doesn't like casserole-type things; he doesn't like things that are out of the ordinary. Ronnie will eat anything. So there are lots of nights if I just say I'm making this then Tim will have to make a choice. But then if he doesn't there will be an occasion where he will just have to make a sandwich or do those things . . . if I don't like something I don't make it, so I feel like my kids should have some opinion and some choice.

Some shoppers must not only take into account children's preferences but also the preferences of extended family members. Karen Calhoun quit work several years ago to stay home with her mother when her mother was diagnosed with Alzheimer's disease. The planning for her most recent shopping trip the morning of the interview involved getting a pen, paper, and the latest grocery ad as she made a list for a couple days worth of meals. When she plans and cooks, she has to keep in mind her mother's needs as well as the needs of her three teen-aged daughters and husband. She said:

> Grandma gets so confused that she might be eating supper at two in the afternoon, so I have to have something ready for her plus now she adds a new dimension to the grocery shopping because she's very, very finicky—now I have to pick and choose things that she will eat as well. Week by week changes because she has forgotten what she liked the week before. Like this week she does like fish, she does like chicken, she will not eat anything that is mixed together like spaghetti, casseroles, anything like that she won't eat, so you have to keep everything separate. Her needs are probably ninety percent of the grocery planning because my family will eat anything, so I have to cook things that she will eat.

In terms of cooking, juggling these needs often structures the timing of meals:

> I usually make dinner about one in the afternoon because then I have Grandma to feed and Jackie will come home next and she'll eat, then Sydney will come home next and she'll eat, and then Doug comes home at seven or eight at night and then he eats. Nobody eats together. We all eat in shifts.

Jackie Engle, a mother of three who runs a home daycare, has to shop for both her family and for her business, so saving money is one of her primary goals. She described her planning work this way:

> We get the ads on Wednesday and I make a list of what is on sale and I really plan it around kind of what's on sale, if it's stuff we like. That sounds crazy but I'm pretty thrifty. Or we attempt to do that. A lot of times we just wing it, though; it gets to be dinner time and we're like "what are we going to have?". . . I've got daycare in my house about twenty days a month so I've got to do the fruit, vegetables, and the main course that we're having since I have to keep up with regulations. So I'm always getting those things and being up on those and then I have to consider my family.

Jackie tries to include other members of the family in making the list, with limited success:

> I have trained my two oldest, meaning my husband and firstborn daughter, to write down things we run out of. Now if we run out of salt, they are not going to tell me, but if it's something they like or their cereal they will write it down. [Do you have a specific list?] Well, we just have a piece of paper we throw over by the phone and they just write it on there. But whose fault is it when they run out? Mom. Because I was supposed to know that they were going to get diarrhea and we were out of Imodium? Who knows, it's just like "how is this my fault?" It would probably do me good to occasionally just wig out and go "this isn't my problem."

Planning also involves taking into account household members' schedules. April Malloy is a full-time worker with two kids who has a two-hour commute every day in addition to being the primary provisioner. Planning for her is not only about meal preparation and eating, but also about scheduling, cooking, and eating around her kids' events. When I asked her about her most recent shopping trip, she recounted:

> I had a list, a little sticky note with just a couple of things. Just a couple things I wanted: some baked chicken already made because I knew I wouldn't have time

to cook tonight and toilet paper. That's really typical. I usually have about five things unless I'm planning for some weekend or something. But yeah, I usually don't buy many things at one time. I also don't do a lot of cooking. I encourage the kids to go to breakfast at school and lunch so really I only have to plan one meal . . . When they have ball practice maybe I'll fix some sandwiches for them to eat on the road and then when I come back I'm going to have a salad or something like that. And Reggie [her husband] can fend for himself or when I get back he'll eat whatever I make him, you know at eight or nine.

Stacey Ostrander, at the time I interviewed her, had just switched from part-time to full-time employment. This shift changed the way she planned for shopping. When she worked part-time, shopping was done in a much less structured way. Now that she works full time:

I spend more time organizing because I go to the store less. I will do a big shop on the weekend and I used to avoid it on the weekend because everybody else was already there and then I would do it in the afternoons. Now, I plan what I am fixing for the week so I know what I need to stock up on and then if I run back into the store it is once, maybe twice. So I actually go to the grocery store less but I have more planning because I sit there and plan out the meals more.

Not only does she plan meals and make lists but she also has to use her time differently as well. While she does her big shopping on the weekend, the trip to pick up missing items has to be scheduled with other activities. She described planning for her smaller trips:

I usually stop at [the supermarket] Thursday afternoons because Gerilyn has a half hour piano lesson. I drop her off at the piano lesson and I have thirty minutes and I've got to be back after those thirty minutes to pick her up, so it can't be a long trip. And you can't get caught in a long line. It has to be efficient; it has to be a short trip and it has to be very specific things that I need and I have to know which things they are. That's usually when I do it because it works out the best. Gerilyn is so tired, when she gets done with everything it will be five fifteen or five twenty and she's been at school since eight. She is ready to come home—she isn't ready to do a grocery shopping trip on the way home from work.

Stacey's daughter has a severe peanut allergy, so part of the grocery planning involves identifying products that her daughter can eat safely.

One couple I interviewed (separately) stood out in that they both were committed to sharing the food work. Colin Moore, a full-time worker, and Meg Moore, a full-time student and instructor, have one child. Because they are so invested in eating and food and have built up a working knowledge of what they like to eat, Colin described their planning as minimal unless they are making something from a recipe and need to make a list:

> We used to plan out the whole week or at least plan enough to make six meals this week and get stuff for that. And then sometimes, though, we kind of have a set list of meals so you can go to the store and know what to get. I usually open the cabinet, open the fridge, see what's there or not there, and then go to the store to fill in the missing spots.

Meg added:

> We usually get the same stuff all the time, so we do a quick scan, check if we are out of this and then unless we are making stuff we don't usually make, like we are following a recipe or something, we don't really need a list. We have a general basic running list. We know what we eat. [It sounds like you communicate a lot about food.] We do it as we shop, too. I ask, "What do you think, should we get two tofus? Are we going to have this two times this week?" So we kind of do it as we go. That is more of our style. Or right before we will kind of scan and say we are low on rice and we only have one can of garbanzo beans, we are good on juice, we need more milk, and we will kind of communicate while we are getting stuff.

Meg and Colin find that shopping together eliminates some of the planning often done prior to the store trip.

DIVISION OF LABOR

How do the other shoppers in the study negotiate the household shopping labor? Many indicate that grocery shopping is *their* responsibility because their partners do not have the skills and knowledge necessary to perform this work. April Malloy, sighing, stated that her husband is a shopping liability: "He will start seeing things [in the store]. He's terrible. He's very spontaneous and wants things as he sees them. It doesn't matter if they are on sale or not."

Some shoppers feel they have to be the primary shoppers because their partners cannot control their impulses and would only buy junk food. Jane Smith, when asked if she did most of the shopping, replied:

Yes, I'd say I do ninety percent. If I send John to the store to get hamburger, we get ice cream, chips, more ice cream. He likes Oreo cookies; I never buy those. He's a fiend for junk food. He will go willingly [to the store] but he doesn't do well with staying on my list . . . it's just easier to do it myself. You think you're going to make tacos, but you don't have any cheese; you have a lot of ice cream.

Lisa Corbin, a mother of four who works part time, said that her husband was not capable of doing the shopping. When asked why, she replied:

He wouldn't get the right kind of apples, or he wouldn't get the right kind of string cheese, or we don't really need that. [The right kind? That your kids like?] Yes, the kind that my kids like, or like just the wrong brands maybe, or he would just determine that we don't really need that or skip that thing. He's never shopped, never been a shopper; it's a difficult thing shopping for a family of six.

Some shoppers articulated that it is difficult for them to share this work with their partners. Tracey Kennedy, a full-time working mother of a pre-schooler, and Kay Worthington, a part-time worker and mother of a teenager, talked about the loss of control they have over what gets purchased if their spouses do the shopping. Tracey said, "I don't mind the shopping most of the time. I feel like I'm in control; I'm making the decisions for the family. I don't like it when Mark wants to do the shopping by himself—it freaks me out. I can't tell if the right decisions are being made."

Kay even connected the choices made at the store to a feeling of power:

Yes, although, you know what, most of our lives even when I was working and even when I was going to school full time, I did the shopping. Probably that is for two reasons: one is he probably has no interest in doing it at all, and two, I was, I am really controlling over what gets bought. There is some power for me. It's very scary for me to send someone to the grocery store not knowing what they are going to bring home. Because I may say apples and they buy the wrong kind . . . I guess I have my ideas of what is best.

Even in households in which both spouses shop for food, women express a greater concern with nutrition and the overall connection between food and health. While Karen Jones, a stay-at-home mother of two young children, says that her husband is as involved with the kids as she is, the work of food shopping is still not quite evenly split because "I get the final word on what we are going to eat or not. It's probably more important to me what goes inside the kids, not that he doesn't want to have healthy food, but he's not going to be as neurotic about the ingredients in everything they eat as I am."

This issue will be discussed at greater length in the next chapter, but Jessica Pierce hints at the problem of feeding in general: "Ian [her spouse] used to cook when he stayed home with our daughter but in order for the children to eat healthy you go ahead and fix the meal for them."

Many of the spouses did shop in some capacity, although most went to the store to get specific items or were provided with lists arranged by the primary shopper. When asked if her spouse did any of the shopping, Stacey Ostrander stated:

> Once in a while. Not very often. If I ask him to stop at the grocery store on the way home, it is for something very specific. It isn't to say please go shopping; it's to say please pick up a gallon of skim milk and a dozen eggs.

Maggie Waggoner's spouse will reluctantly shop, but only for a few items:

> I do all the planning. I do all the thinking of what we need. I will call him and say, "Can you pick up a couple things and if it's more than two then it has to go on a list because you don't remember." He will go pick up a few items, but if the list gets too big then he doesn't want any part of it. He does not like the grocery experience at all. He doesn't like the shopping experience at all. He wants to go in and grab the milk and leave.

Karen Calhoun sends her husband with a list so he can shop after work in the larger town:

> Dan goes shopping once I make out the list and tell him exactly what to get and then he checks it off when he gets that item. But he does a fine job of it. He does my Aldi's list because he is in [the city] so the things that I know that I can get cheaper like fresh produce and milk he gets at Aldi's.

Only a few spouses refuse to participate in the shopping process. When I asked April if her husband went shopping, she replied:

> Maybe once a month when I've gone on strike and don't want to go shopping and he is finally starving enough to get out there, but yeah, he doesn't unless there

is nothing to eat. He thinks that it's my job and my purpose in life to bring the groceries in.

She recounted a story about a recent shopping strike she went on when the household was out of toilet paper. She was waiting for her husband to go to the store to buy the toilet paper, but when the standoff lasted for several days she finally broke down and bought it herself.

Even the one couple who shops together has to divide the labor at times. Although they try to shop as a family, Colin's hour-and-a-half daily commute sometimes makes it difficult. Meg said:

> We like to do stuff together, so Saturdays we try to stick together and do this kind of work. But sometimes I end up doing it on my own because it's just been a busy week or we are out of stuff. Or if our Saturday gets taken up by something else, then I'll end up doing it Monday with Laurie [her daughter].

AT THE STORE

Grocery shopping at the supermarket is ostensibly a standardized process. Once the shopper has reached the parking lot, the design of the store ushers her through the automatic doors, where she grabs her shopping cart and then follows the layout of the store (first produce, then meats/dairy, grocery, breads), chooses products from the shelf, which she places in the cart, and eventually wheels all these items to the cash register. Some stores require customers to bag their own groceries or even use self-checkout. Once unloaded from the car, the groceries are stored in pantries until needed for meals. As we talked with shoppers, however, we found significant variations in how individuals experience this process.

For the three shoppers who didn't have children or were retired, the work of shopping was much more flexible. They spent much less time planning meals and expressed less anxiety about feeding issues when only one or two people were in the household. They also had more flexibility in timing their shopping trip; they had fewer schedules to work around, were not required to make meals at a certain time, and could even decide to eat out more often.

Jill Burnett, a single woman with no children, described her shopping trips as "getting what I need and what I like." She rarely makes a list and spends less than twenty minutes in the grocery store on her way home from work. One of her most pressing shopping issues is buying the right amount of food:

> I don't buy a bag of potatoes; I buy a couple potatoes because I won't even eat them up before they are no good. You know, a bag of chicken breasts, I have to think long and hard whether I'm going to buy them because I think, "Will they go bad before I eat them up? Or will it get dried up with freezer burn or whatever?" So I typically don't buy large quantities of things like that. I'll buy a couple chicken breasts. I think about a package of hot dogs. I'm never going to eat the whole package before it goes bad, so I do throw away food because it will go bad in my fridge.

On the other end of the spectrum is the stay-at-home mother of two who spends the most time shopping of anyone in the study. Karen Jones stated that food is very important not only for health but also for connection:

> I try to incorporate everybody as much as I possibly can. I try to eat the food, I try to grow my own food, I try to show the kids where the food is coming from as much as I can, so if I can have interaction with the farmer or if I can have interaction with the baker that we do, and still, furthermore, because what we eat is so important, we kind of go as a family. That's a big part of our lives, probably one of the major parts of how I raise my kids or how our family connects.

She shops in many different venues and maintains a garden in the back yard. There is no separate "grocery trip"; purchasing food is part of their weekly routine:

> We normally go to the farmers' market on Saturday and then on Sunday we go shopping; either Sunday or Monday we go shopping at the local health store and because the [supermarket] is only a couple blocks away, we go over there, probably every other day or something. We don't do a big shopping trip. We get our bread at the baker's and we'll ride our bikes to the baker's once a week probably. So food buying is a huge part of what we do.

She did acknowledge, however, that if she were working full time, her shopping work would be different. She stated, "It would be real different, I would think. I would not be going all the time. But because I'm home and can do that, I do it."

Shopping is also experienced differently depending on how many people the shopper must take with her. Negotiating shopping with kids was a frequent topic of discussion among the shoppers in my study. Jackie Engle said:

I try to escape my three children. And try to go without them. Honestly, because if I take my kids I spend ten dollars more just because they all have an opinion about what they want. But there were days when they were tiny and Ron [her spouse] was coaching, I had three kids in car seats, not just booster seats, with coats in the winter and you might only need two things, but you still had to take them all and that's the hard stuff.

I asked Lisa Corbin if she takes her kids shopping with her. She replied:

Yeah, my kids are always with me. I try to make them help. I ask them to pick out a couple of good apples, pick out the macaroni and cheese that we want, that kind of thing, but the baby is the worst. [Have you found any strategies for him?] No, I just let him scream. I used to think, "How could mothers let their kids scream like that?" But now I am *that* woman. I let him scream . . . It's an exhausting experience, physically and mentally.

Colin Moore usually goes shopping with his spouse and child. He said his daughter usually rides in the cart and he "hands her stuff and she reads the names of it and puts it in the cart." If he didn't give her something to do, she would be "eyeing stuff and saying, 'I want this. I want that.'"

Karen Jones believes that a huge part of her shopping effort is managing her two-year-old and four-year-old during the shopping trip. She said:

When we are at the [supermarket] they get a book or hold a toy or are engaged in some kind of I spy game. There is something going with them so they are engaged or playing with me. Occasionally my daughter will help me shop by going down the aisles and getting whatever it is I need . . . Evelyn is a toddler and isn't old enough to play those kinds of games, and I have to keep her entertained as much as I can, which is a large part of what I do at the store.

Even the physical act of shopping is much more difficult for some shoppers than others. The discount store is a warehouse box store designed for large shopping trips. For some shoppers, including single mothers with kids and the elderly, this configuration requires extra physical work including walking from the huge parking lot in front of the store, getting kids into the cart or keeping them occupied, having to walk through much of the cavernous store even if for a few items, sacking the groceries, and carrying them out and loading them into the car.

For a single mother in my study who has two boys, a two-year-old and a six-year-old who uses a wheelchair, shopping becomes a marathon. To negotiate the store itself, Peggy uses one hand to push the cart and the other hand to pull the wheelchair. Because she is unemployed at this time and is on a strict budget, she sometimes takes a calculator and stops after each product is put in the cart to calculate the total amount. After she loads all her products on the conveyer belt, she bags her own groceries and then has to negotiate the parking lot. She tries to park near a cart corral, because she doesn't like to leave the kids in the car while she takes the cart back. This is her description of getting both the groceries and the kids in the car:

> Sometimes if it's not real bad out I will sit there and I will leave the kids sitting outside and I will load everything and I will push the cart and pull Teddy and I will take the cart up there and then carry Ken on my hip and push Teddy's wheelchair back to the van because I don't like leaving them sit there.

At the end of a shopping trip she is "totally exhausted."

CONCLUSION

Food provisioning has long been considered women's work, often requiring women to grow their own food, to employ other women to shop and cook in their stead, or to purchase food at the market. Changes in transportation, energy use, and residential patterns have all contributed to the contemporary nature of grocery shopping. The physical work of food provisioning, once a visible and daily activity, is now confined mainly to periodic trips to the grocery store. However, much invisible labor is also necessary for this work to get done, including menu planning and list making, accounting for household needs and schedules, negotiating with partners and dependents, and knowing what is available to purchase at the store and what is good to eat.

For the people in my study, shopping was an activity still mediated by gender. Although some shoppers shared the cooking and shopping with their spouses, all women in my study assumed management for the shopping and cooking work. How these shoppers accomplished the tasks of shopping and cooking often depended on their relationship to wage-earning work. Women who worked full time spent much less time planning and cooking and used greater convenience foods such as eating out or prepared deli meals to feed their families. However, they still assumed responsibility for getting that food home and arranging schedules. Women who worked part time or stayed at home spent more time planning, making meal plans, and cooking at home, as well as shopping.

We also hear in the words of the shoppers a certain knowledge of how to shop that is culturally and historically specific and that shapes the activity of shopping and provisioning their families. These shoppers complain that they cannot send their husbands to the store because they will often buy junk foods or foods that only they will like, they rarely shop with the household or children's nutrition in mind, and they are often unaware of the necessity of strategies of shopping that will save money. Shoppers also indicate that they know the best way to plan, they know what their kids will eat—in other words, they know the best way to shop.

How do these women know what is the right way to shop? Much of their shopping knowledge is based on their own experience, but it is also shaped by institutional forces that can be discerned from their description of their work and from the texts that guide that work. In the next three chapters, we will hear more from shoppers and managers about their experiences in relation to saving money, nutrition, and how the grocery store environment is constructed. In these descriptions we can then illuminate institutional discourses that shape how the activity of grocery shopping is structured.

—3—

Shopping and the Nutrition Discourse

In the previous chapter, we saw that grocery shopping involves many activities and skills. Starting with the work of these shoppers and the language they use to describe it, the next two chapters investigate how this work is shaped by texts and discourses that originate in the work of experts in the larger institutional food complex, which includes journalists, nutritionists, government agents, and industry representatives. In this chapter, I give examples of one textually based discourse and show how this discourse affects the choices of working-class and middle-class shoppers in different ways. Ultimately, the discourse that standardizes the knowledge of nutrition, which I call the individual responsibility for nutrition, makes all shoppers accountable for the health of the individuals in their household.

Almost all shoppers talked about nutrition, and many shoppers expressed significant concerns about nutrition and the health of their families in relationship to the work they do in grocery shopping. Jackie Engle told me:

> I do try to cook stuff that's low fat and stuff like that. I'm not a big sugar worrier and I should be more. My kids can have Post Toasties with sugar and something else on it and I don't even care. I should. I should worry more about that, but they are eating and they are having milk . . . My kids are not real vegetable people and that's my fault because we didn't probably push them enough when they were little. I should have really shoved the vegetables at them so it would be better.

Jackie knows that her family should not eat sugar or fat and should eat more vegetables; she is implicitly referring to some kind of institutional knowledge about what is good and healthy. But she lets her kids eat sugared cereal, she only buys certain fat-free foods, and she does not require her children to eat vegetables. She doesn't experiment much with the family meals, but she does realize that she is accountable for her children's nutrition and thus their health—when she states "it would be better" she means that she would fulfill her responsibility as food provider if she lived up to these standards and her kids would somehow be healthier.

Tracey Kennedy knows that her family is supposed to eat more fruits and vegetables but encountered this dilemma over broccoli:

> Should you put the fattening ranch on it to get them to eat the vitamins? I don't know what the answer is. I guess I know what we are doing to get the vitamins from the broccoli and at least cultivate some getting it down them versus no vegetable at all. I'm ambivalent but that's what we are going with. And here we use a lighter ranch with reduced fat and again I don't know what the long-term consequences of those things are.

Her ambivalence is related to her connection with expert nutrition knowledge that stresses low-fat foods and high intakes of fruits and vegetables. But what about the dislikes and desires of the individuals eating the food? It is the shoppers' responsibility to reconcile their local relationships and experiences with this nutrition information.

Maggie Waggoner has battled her weight for many years and worries that her kids will have the same issues. One of her biggest nutritional concerns is the amount of fat in her family's diet. She gave these examples:

> I am really into watching the nutrition value of food and I do watch what kinds of food we have. Walmart has this really good brand of breaded chicken breasts; they are frozen and are all ready just to microwave them or whatever, and I justify buying them [because] they are like seven or eight grams of fat per chicken patty, well, most brands are like thirty grams of fat. I get chicken rings that are like two grams of fat per serving. We do a lot of frozen French fries because you have to check your brands. Some have eight to ten grams of fat per serving, but then there are those that have two to three. And so we throw them on the George Foreman about twice a week; my kids love it. My husband is like, "These kids eat too many French fries" and I'm like, "Two grams of fat? A baked potato is going to have more grams of fat because you are going to be putting butter and whatever on them."

She does try to have fresh fruit on the table every night and most nights also a fresh vegetable. While she does try to keep healthy food in the house, she confessed that she also buys junk: "You know, last night I brought home Oreo cookies."

Since she also tries to limit calories, she drinks diet pop. Her kids also drink diet soda due to weight concerns and cavity issues. But even this causes concern, as she stated:

> But there are people who are looking at me and go, "You should not be giving kids diet pop." But they get one diet pop a day, one artificial sweetener a day. And that's another one of my things, what's better for you? Is sugar any better for you than sweetener?

While food safety is another significant issue for her, overall, she is most concerned about her kids' diet. She spends time shopping and preparing the foods she thinks are important for her kids to eat, and expends emotional energy thinking and worrying about what they eat. She stated:

> I would never have worried about all that [nutrition] before the kids . . . I don't think I was always such a worried, obsessive person about when it comes to food, but I think I've always been that way when it comes to my kids.

NUTRITION KNOWLEDGE

Shoppers do not see, smell, or taste fat, calories, or sugar grams; these concepts are not known from experience but are based on knowledge disseminated through discourses created at extra-local institutional sites. For institutional ethnographers, this signals an institutional knowledge that goes beyond the everyday lived experience. Shoppers did not know these terms intuitively; they had to acquire this knowledge from outside their experience. The second step in the institutional ethnography process is to identify texts that influence our everyday work. In the case of grocery shopping, the people I interviewed identified and referenced texts such as women's magazines (*More*, *Simple Living*, *Good Housekeeping*), television news shows (*Good Morning America*, *Today Show*), local news shows, newspapers, government agencies (U.S. Department of Agriculture, Health and Human Services), medical brochures, and store advertisements as sources of information about food shopping and nutrition.

Analyzing these sources for shopping information, it did not take long to identify a certain approach to nutrition. The main message of this nutrition discourse is that the most important aspect of food is the individual nutrients, and once these are quantified we can develop a numerical literacy to make our food choices. Writers and scholars have discussed and critiqued this reductionist process in much more depth (Dixon and Banwell 2004; Mudry 2009; Nestle 2002; Pollan 2007), but the main criteria for choosing food rests on numbers: How many calories? How many grams of fat? How many milligrams of salt?

Nearly all contemporary shoppers are familiar with the basics of nutrition knowledge, having been introduced either to the four food groups or the food pyramid in both its early 1980s manifestation and the newer MyPyramid version. The antecedent to the food pyramid, the four basic food groups, was the basis of U.S. food policy until the mid-1970s (Nestle 2002). This policy instructed individuals to eat from the four basic food groups—milk, meat, vegetables and fruits, and breads and cereals—to ensure that they received the right balance of nutrients (Nestle 2002).

Mainstream nutrition and dietary information is directly based on federal recommendations delineated in "The Dietary Guidelines for Americans," a joint publication of the U.S. Department of Health and Human Services and the U.S. Department of Agriculture. After I had finished the data collection for this project, the Dietary Guidelines were updated to include a more targeted focus on exercise; however, much of the focus on food through science was retained. For example, the 2005 Guidelines' stated purpose is to provide "a science-based advice to promote health and to reduce risk for major chronic diseases through diet and physical activity" (U.S. Department of Health and Human Services 2005a), while the goal of the 2010 report is "to summarize and synthesize knowledge about individual nutrients and food components into an interrelated set of recommendations for healthy eating that can be adopted by the public" (U.S. Department of Health and Human Services 2010).

A good example of this quantified approach to food is found in the executive summary of the 2010 Guidelines. This document encourages consumers to reduce consumption of certain foods and to increase consumption of other foods, always using a scientific and reductionist justification. For example, consumers are instructed to:

Figure 3.1 MyPyramid logo.
Source: U.S. Department of Health and Human Services 2010.

- Consume less than 10 percent of calories from saturated fatty acids by replacing them with monounsaturated and polyunsaturated fatty acids.
- Consume less than 300 mg per day of dietary cholesterol.
- Keep *trans* fatty acid consumption as low as possible by limiting foods that contain synthetic sources of *trans* fats, such as partially hydrogenated oils, and by limiting other solid fats.
- Reduce the intake of calories from solid fats and added sugars.
- Limit the consumption of foods that contain refined grains, especially refined grain foods that contain solid fats, added sugars, and sodium.

The instructions regarding the foods and nutrients we should increase include:

- Consume at least half of all grains as whole grains. Increase whole grain intake by replacing refined grains with whole grains.

· Replace protein foods that are higher in solid fats with choices that are lower in solid fats and calories and/or are sources of oils.
· Use oils to replace solid fats where possible.
· Choose foods that provide more potassium, dietary fiber, calcium, and vitamin D, which are nutrients of concern in American diets. These foods include vegetables, fruits, whole grains, and milk and milk products (U.S. Department of Health and Human Services 2010).

The new MyPlate icon attempted to simplify this nutrition information by representing food proportionally on a plate; that is, fruits and vegetables should take up half the plate, with more vegetables than fruits and grains and proteins should comprise the other half. However, when reading the category guidelines in the larger USDA/HHS document, the recommendations revert back to quantification (see Table 3.1). Not only should we eat more fruits and vegetables than other foods, but we should adjust our intake (as measured in cups) by gender and age. Imagine using this chart to plan a week's worth of dinners for a family of four!

One way to make sure we are eating the right foods in the right amount is to use the nutrition label to help us make decisions.

Table 3.1 Food Groups: Vegetables

		Dark Green Vegetables	Orange Vegetables	Dry Beans and Peas	Starchy Vegetables	Other Vegetables
Children	2–3 years old	1 cup	½ cup	½ cup	1 ½ cups	4 cups
	4–8 years old	1 ½ cups	1 cup	1 cup	2 ½ cups	4 ½ cups
Girls	9–13 years old	2 cups	1 ½ cups	2 ½ cups	2 ½ cups	5 ½ cups
	14–18 years old	3 cups	2 cups	3 cups	3 cups	6 ½ cups
Boys	9–13 years old	3 cups	2 cups	3 cups	3 cups	6 ½ cups
	14–18 years old	3 cups	2 cups	3 cups	6 cups	7 cups
Women	19–30 years old	3 cups	2 cups	3 cups	3 cups	6 ½ cups
	31–50 years old	3 cups	2 cups	3 cups	3 cups	6 ½ cups
	51+ years old	2 cups	1 ½ cups	2 ½ cups	2 ½ cups	5 ½ cups
Men	19–30 years old	3 cups	2 cups	3 cups	6 cups	7 cups
	31–50 years old	3 cups	2 cups	3 cups	6 cups	7 cups
	51+ years old	3 cups	2 cups	3 cups	3 cups	6 ½ cups

Source: U.S. Department of Agriculture 2010b.

Nutrition Facts

Serving Size 1 cup (228g)
Servings Per Container 2

Amount Per Serving

Calories 250   Calories from Fat 110

	% **Daily Value***
Total Fat 12g	18%
Saturated Fat 3g	15%
Trans Fat 3g	
Cholesterol 30mg	10%
Sodium 470mg	20%
Potassium 700mg	20%
Total Carbohydrate 31g	10%
Dietary Fiber 0g	0%
Sugars 5g	
Protein 5g	

Vitamin A	4%
Vitamin C	2%
Calcium	20%
Iron	4%

* Percent Daily Values are based on a 2,000 calorie diet.
Your Daily Values may be higher or lower depending on
your calorie needs.

	Calories:	2,000	2,500
Total fat	Less than	65g	80g
Sat fat	Less than	20g	25g
Cholesterol	Less than	300mg	300mg
Sodium	Less than	2,400mg	2,400mg
Total Carbohydrate		300g	375g
Dietary Fiber		25g	30g

Figure 3.2   How to read the nutrition label.
Source: U.S. Food and Drug Administration 2006.

This label should be read in the following manner, according to the U.S. Food and Drug Administration (2006):

- The % Daily Value is a key to a balanced diet. The % DV is a general guide to help you link nutrients in a serving of food to their contribution to your total daily diet. It can help you determine if a food is high or low in a nutrient—5% or less is low, 20% or more is high. You can use the % DV to make dietary trade-offs with other foods throughout the day. The * is a re-minder that the % DV is based on a 2,000-calorie diet. You may need more or less, but the % DV is still a helpful gauge.
- Check the serving size and number of servings. The Nutrition Facts Label information is based on ONE serving, but many packages contain more. Look at the serving size and how many servings you are actually consum-ing. If you double the servings you eat, you double the calories and nutri-ents, including the % DVs.
- Look for foods that are rich in these nutrients. Use the label not only to limit fat and sodium, but also to increase nutrients that promote good health and may protect you from disease. Some Americans don't get enough vitamins A and C, potassium, calcium, and iron, so choose the brand with the higher % DV for these nutrients. Get the most nutrition for your calories—compare the calories to the nutrients you would be getting to make a healthier food choice.
- Know your fats and reduce sodium for your health. To help reduce your risk of heart disease, use the label to select foods that are lowest in saturated fat, trans fat and cholesterol. Trans fat doesn't have a % DV, but consume as little as possible because it increases your risk of heart disease. The % DV for total fat includes all different kinds of fats. To help lower blood cholesterol, replace saturated and trans fats with monounsaturated and polyunsaturated fats found in fish, nuts, and liquid vegetable oils. Limit sodium to help reduce your risk of high blood pressure.
- Reach for healthy, wholesome carbohydrates. Fiber and sugars are types of carbohydrates. Healthy sources, like fruits, vegetables, beans, and whole grain, can reduce the risk of heart disease and improve digestive function-ing. Whole grain foods can't always be identified by color or name, such as multi-grain or wheat. Look for the "whole" grain listed first in the ingredient list, such as whole wheat, brown rice, or whole oats. There isn't a % DV for

sugar, but you can compare the sugar content in grams among products. Limit foods with added sugars (sucrose, glucose, fructose, corn or maple syrup), which add calories but not other nutrients, such as vitamins and minerals. Make sure that added sugars are not one of the first few items in the ingredients list. For protein, choose foods that are lower in fat. Most Americans get plenty of protein, but not always from the healthiest sources. When choosing a food for its protein content, such as meat, poultry, dry beans, milk and milk products, make choices that are lean, low-fat, or fat free.

While this nutrition information is ostensibly designed to educate the shopper, it concomitantly makes her responsible for acquiring this information and holds her accountable for the consequences of ignoring the information or not using it correctly.

INSTITUTIONAL AGENTS

This discourse has powerful agents that support and disseminate this information. The United States Department of Agriculture is the leading governmental organization for nutrition information and includes several agencies that propose and support nutrition research, policy, and education, including the Center for Nutrition Policy and Promotion (CNPP), the Food and Nutrition Service, and the Cooperative State Research and Education (CSREES) agency. The CSREES, for example, is also connected to land grant institutions and the extension offices that operate under these universities. Cooperative extension offices are county agencies staffed by experts who, according to their website, "provide useful, practical, and research-based information to agricultural producers, small business owners, youth, consumers, and others in rural areas and communities of all sizes." The experts employed at these agencies have degrees in agriculture and family and consumer sciences education, which also includes diet and nutrition.

The U.S. Department of Health and Human Services also has a stake in grocery shopping advice, especially as it relates to health. One aspect of this department's mission listed on its website is "protecting the health of all Americans," and services include health and social science research and preventing disease by providing immunization services and assuring food and drug safety. Under the HHS umbrella are the Centers for Disease Control (CDC), National Institutes of Health (NIH), and the Food and Drug Administration (FDA). The HHS publication, *A Healthier You: Based on the Dietary Guidelines for Americans*, is based on nutrition policy developed under the Center for Nutrition Policy and Promotion at the USDA and is a joint publication between the HHS and the Office of Disease and Health Promotion. The main message in several of their publications is that "Healthy eating is associated with reduced risk for many diseases, including the three leading causes of death: heart disease, cancer, and stroke" (U.S. Department of Health and Human Services 2005a). These agencies base their nutrition information on the food pyramid, while also emphasizing the connection between food and disease.

The Academy of Nutrition and Dietetics (AND), formerly the American Dietetic Association, is another institutional agent involved in the dissemination of health and nutrition information. Comprised of registered dieticians and nutritionists, this organization's shopping and food information is based on the food pyramid and has cross references to the USDA and CNPP websites. Its stated goal is "to improve the nation's health and advance the profession of dietetics . . . by providing reliable and evidence-based Nutrition information to the public" (www.eatright.org/about).

These agencies are all concerned with pressing social problems and have many employees who work diligently to confront malnutrition, poverty, and a host of other social issues in addition to researching and teaching about nutrition. However, the nutrition discourse often makes it difficult to personalize solutions and becomes even more entrenched when connected to larger retail and manufacturing organizations.

Some of the Academy of Nutrition and Dietetics publications for consumers were sponsored by large agro-food companies. For example, the "Nutrition Fact Sheet: Dietary Fats: Clarifying an Age-Old Issue" is sponsored by the Promise Institute, an organization under the umbrella of Unilever (the company that makes Promise Buttery spreads). The nutritional message from this publication is that "To maintain heart health, the best choice is to reduce both saturated and trans fat by replacing butter, lard, and shortening and hard stick margarine with unsaturated fats such as soft, non-hydrogenated margarine and vegetable oils like olive, canola, sunflower and soybean oils" (American Dietetic Association 2006c). Interestingly, the Promise spread happens to fit these guidelines.

If consumers have more questions, they can go to the Promise Institute website and send an e-mail message to a staff dietician. Unilever is also introducing an Eat Smart logo, discussed on its website, to "help customers make healthier choices amongst our products. Because shoppers are so busy and reducing the amount of trans fat, saturated fats, sugars and sodium is so important to health and overall well-being, Unilever has made it easy to chose food items that meet specific Unilever criteria which are based on U.S. Dietary Guidelines" (www.unilver.com).

Other food industry corporations are involved in promoting the nutrition discourse. Wendy's, the fast food restaurant chain, sponsored a Fact Sheet on the AND website titled "Eating Better Together: A Family Guide for a Healthier Lifestyle," in which a section of the two-page brochure is devoted to tips for choosing a restaurant when "on the go" (American Dietetic Association 2006a). One of the bulleted points is to "select colorful fruits and vegetables like spinach, tomatoes and mandarin oranges." At the time this fact sheet was published in 2005, Wendy's was the only fast food chain to include fruit, specifically mandarin oranges, in children's meals. Wendy's also has a website titled "Mom˜RD" that connects moms with registered dieticians.

Retail stores are also promoting the government's guidelines on food and nutrition in several ways. Albertson's, a large supermarket chain, is offering personalized MyPyramid information on making "healthy choices for their families" by having shoppers punch in their age, weight, height, and level of physical activity at store kiosks (standing computers). This information can be used to purchase food items based on these recommendations. Aisle markers and shelf tags are color coded to help shoppers locate specific categories in their personal food pyramid (Zwiebach 2007). Retailers are also adding dieticians to their staffs who can offer customers nutrition and healthy lifestyle information (Lempert 2007b). Hy-Vee has dieticians at the corporate level whom customers can contact on its website with particular health and wellness questions.

EXAMPLES OF NUTRITION DISCOURSE

Information about food and health abounds in the media. Morning and local news shows, women's magazines, and websites such as Weight Watchers, all feature nutrition and health information on a daily basis. An article from *Good Housekeeping* titled "The ABCs of Vitamin D" provides a good illustration of the nutrition discourse described above, which reduces health to the consumption of individual nutrients based on scientific knowledge:

> Take a close look at the label on your multi: Unless the vitamin D is listed as D3 (or cholecalciferol) you're getting shortchanged. Some bills contain D2 (ergocalciferol) once thought to be equivalent to D3 but now proven to be "substantially less potent," says Reinhold Vieth, Ph.D., director of the Bone and Mineral Laboratory at Mount Sinai Hospital. Low vitamin D blood levels have been linked to a host of health problems, from osteoporosis to several cancers. Many experts advise all adults to get about 1,000 IU of D daily, whether from supplements or fortified foods, including milk and yogurt. (Hammock 2007)

Another example of the issue of fruits and vegetables that speaks to the dilemma of the mother listed above is found in *Parade Magazine*. The article asks, "why is it so important to eat more servings of fruits and vegetables?" The answer:

> Fruits and vegetables are full of good stuff—such as fiber, antioxidants, vitamins and minerals—that helps to reduce your risk of certain cancers and many chronic diseases, including diabetes. Unfortunately, more than 90% of us don't get the recommended average of 10 servings of fruits and vegetables in our daily diets. Here are a few examples of single servings from the Department of Agriculture: a medium fruit (such as an apple or banana); a half cup of chopped, cooked or canned fruit or vegetables; or 4 ounces of juice. (O'Shea 2007)

Even the local food cooperative advertisement includes information on the nutrients in its food. This advertisement features acai, a type of fruit grown in the Amazon rain forest. The ad states:

> [I]t has a rich berry-cocoa flavor, is packed with more antioxidants than blueberries or pomegranates, and contains loads of healthy Omega fats, protein and dietary fiber. (*The Coop Advantage* May 2008)

Morning news shows often contain nutrition information. Joy Bauer is the nutritionist for *The Today Show* and supports a newsletter with nutrition information. An example of short articles on nutrition information is "Myth and Fact about Brown Sugar," where she concludes:

Blackstrap molasses in particular is a nutritional powerhouse. One tablespoon contains 177 milligrams calcium, 3.6 grams iron, and 510 milligrams potassium. Problem is, the stuff tastes pretty nasty and would definitely not be a good sugar alternative in your morning coffee. Bottom line, minimize all sweeteners, including sugar (white and brown), molasses, and even honey. (Bauer 2012)

Articles and pamphlets often suggest that one way to control the nutrients our household members eat is to make meals at home. One magazine article stated:

One way around the "obesogenic" environment is to eat at home, where you can control both portion sizes and the content of meals. Families who eat out a lot tend to consume fewer fruits and vegetables, nutrition researchers at St. Louis University found. ("The No-Diet Diet" 2005)

Research from Harvard Medical School on the relationship between family meals and obesity is often cited. Eating dinner at home is associated with more healthful dietary intake patterns, including more fruits and vegetables, less fried food and soda, and less saturated and trans fat (Gillman et al. 2000). A pamphlet from The National Center on Addiction and Substance Abuse at Columbia University called "Family Day" offers scientific studies showing that not only are family dinners healthier, they reduce children's risk of substance abuse.

A 2007 study investigated the effect of watching TV on dietary intake of adolescents. While watching TV is associated with poorer dietary quality, boys and girls who watched TV during regular family meals were more likely to report a healthier diet than those who ate alone (Feldman et al. 2007). The authors of this report gave several possible explanations. Families who eat together are more likely to try to prepare well-balanced, nutritious meals and parents have more opportunity to observe dietary behaviors and correct them. Overall, "study findings provide clear evidence for the role of the family meal in enhancing dietary quality among adolescents" (Feldman et al. 2007: 262). The Let's Move website sponsored by Michelle Obama includes eating family meals together as a chance to model good behavior and to provide structure for good eating habits.

In one Pennsylvania school district, children are measured and weighed at school and their BMI numbers are sent home with their report cards because "families do not generally have an accurate perception of the issue" (Kantor 2007). Parents are responsible for their children's BMI score in the same way that they are for their grade card. An Associated Press article on nutrition education argued that parents have the greatest influence over what their kids eat. Parents, then, especially mothers, are to blame if kids are fat. The article quotes Dr. Robert Trevino of the Social and Health Research Center in San Antonio, who states: "If the mother is eating Cheetos and white bread, the fetus will be born with those taste buds. If the mother is eating carrots and oatmeal the child will be born with those taste buds" (Mendoza 2007).

Thus, the nutrition discourse is a science-based approach to eating that breaks food down into constituent parts and makes it the individual shoppers' responsibility to choose these nutrients wisely not only for themselves but for their families and households. This quantitative approach to nutrition attempts to standardize the work of shopping. All shoppers should be looking for the same amounts of food nutrients. All shoppers now must be familiar with this knowledge and shop toward its dictates. But it is specifically the mother's responsibility to provide the right combinations to her children (even in utero) and in doing so create the "proper" family. This approach, however, ignores the real-life constraints that many shoppers face. Examining the work of the shoppers and listening to how they describe what they do allows us to see the work involved in trying to balance the demands of this discourse with their real-life experiences.

SHOPPING FOR NUTRITION

All of the shoppers who participated in my study indicated some knowledge of the nutrition discourse, but middle-class shoppers intimately connected with nutrition texts (and alternative nutrition discourses as well) expressed a much higher level of anxiety concerning the food they were buying for their family than working-class shoppers. This finding parallels other research (DeVault 1991; Dixon 1999) that found working-class shoppers more often draw on experience and tradition for their nutrition knowledge, whereas in the professional middle class, science and style are prized over experience (DeVault 1991: 221).

The working-class shoppers in my study, those who had attained at least a high school diploma and/or had taken college courses, acknowledged some familiarity with the nutrition discourse but didn't express serious concerns about nutrition and even downplayed some of the "expert" information. One of Jane Smith's daughters has kidney stones and she used to read labels to watch for sodium. But now, Jane stated, "We don't worry too much. If I'm making tacos, you know, whatever is in it, is in it."

She did acknowledge aspects of the nutrition discourse but then rejected it using the efficiency discourse (discussed in the next chapter). She said:

> We probably should be reading labels. I think we'd all be healthier for it. But I figure if you need sour cream you need sour cream. Why pay a dollar more for something that says "fat free" and then you find out that the fat free thing gives you cancer anyway. Just give me the fat and we'll call it good.

She also pointed out what to her seem like absurdities:

> I saw on the news last night if you eat enough vitamin D you won't get cancer. But you have to drink a gallon of milk a day to get the benefits. Now I thought, "who is going to do that? Who is going to drink a gallon of milk every single day to not get cancer?"

Another working-class mother, Karen Calhoun, fixes traditional casseroles for her three daughters and her husband—many of the same dishes that she grew up with. She is caring for her mother with Alzheimer's in her home, and now that her mom cannot have any food touching (which precludes casseroles), Karen has had to branch out into meatloaf or chicken dishes or even fish. She tries new recipes from *Taste of Home*, a magazine which features recipes sent in by readers and are what Karen called "tried and true, the best for families." In terms of healthy foods like whole grains, she stated that "stuff like that might be better but it's costlier too because anything that is healthy for you they always jack up the price of it. I don't get that technical." She does read labels sometimes but "more times it's stuff that is new and I'm sure it would be quite an eye opening experience to read the stuff we normally get. But you are always in a hurry, always busy and before you know it you are off to the next thing." Overall, although she does acknowledge some acquaintance with nutrition information, she is not convinced enough by its value to alter her eating or shopping patterns.

When I asked Peggy Fiske, a single mom with two kids, if she had any food or nutrition concerns, she stated that she had read something on Walmart.com about bird flu and she was worried because she had just bought a whole turkey and didn't want to have to throw it away. She knew that there are guidelines to keep people from getting sick, but she stated that, when she buys fresh vegetables and fruits, "I clean them before I fix them," and she makes sure that she doesn't buy any produce with cracks in it that could let in bacteria.

One of Peggy's main concerns is her son getting "real" food to eat. His doctor and a nursing company advised her that he should drink at least three cans of Pedia-sure a day, which they raised to six cans a day. Peggy said that her son has to have the Pedia-sure "to make sure he gets enough nutrients and that's calories and I don't know." She said:

> He had a problem with reflux. And then they kept raising the amount of Pedia-sure he was getting and you know first he was getting sick every time he ate and then he didn't even have an appetite because he was getting six cans a day of Pedia-sure and he was about three years old, so basically I'm having to re-teach him how to eat and trying to remind him "you used to love this." And so it's kind of trying to rebuild his palate because I don't want him on a liquid diet forever.

She worried less about the specific nutrients, but had to contend with experts telling her how many cans of Pedia-sure her son had to have:

> We used to have a nursing company that gave him two or three cans a day and they were wanting him to gain like two pounds a week. I was like, you know, if he continuously gains two pounds a week, he's going to be overweight very quickly and he was holding steady at his weight. And they were just, "He's not gaining any weight. We need to raise the number of cans." And they really pushed for it and I was being overridden and so the doctor wrote up the order. You know nobody was wanting to let me get my two cents in.

Finally, she got his doctor to agree to decrease the number of cans as long as his weight held steady, which it has for several months.

Lisa Corbin has a bachelor's degree and is currently working part time from home. When she talked about shopping for her husband and four children, she acknowledged a familiarity with nutrition, but argued that since her kids were home with her she could control what they ate. She said:

> Nutritionally I wish I made things more from scratch because I know that packaged food is very fattening. But we eat wheat bread, I try to get calcium in a lot of

our food because a couple of my kids don't drink any milk at all. They don't like it. So I try to make sure they are getting enough calcium in other things, like fortified orange juice, and I look for frozen waffles that have calcium. We don't eat sweets a lot, so the snacks that we have are granola bars and yogurt, not candy. We never go to the store and buy just candy. We eat healthy cereal; we don't buy sugared cereal. So I'm not terribly, terribly concerned because I just try to only buy chips about once a month. That means that I'm really not concerned a lot about what they are eating because I know that what they are eating is mainly good for them. Then I figure that as long as they are active, I'm not really concerned about the fat in food, because I think that kids need some fat anyway and I just think that if they are active enough they will be fine.

Middle-class shoppers with higher levels of education, especially professionals committed to expert discourses about food, express significantly more anxiety about what they are eating and especially what they are buying for their kids. They have higher standards for what food they eat and emphasize the health issue of food as a strong variable in their food selection (as well as the ability to pay for it). Kay Worthington stated that she

would never buy something that we wouldn't normally eat. Like any of the ready-made, like Kraft macaroni and cheese, or something like that, we don't eat that kind of stuff and I wouldn't even buy it if it was ten cents apiece because I would worry about the nutritional aspect. I worry about this constantly. Every facet of it . . . I mean honestly the end point of the whole nutritional discussion is that you will die or get sick if you don't eat the certain healthiest stuff. I believe it in my gut.

Kay spends almost $900 a month on food, making sure she buys the freshest and most healthful products, and she is the primary household meal preparer. She goes shopping every couple of days because she worries about produce staying fresh and losing its nutrition if it stays in the refrigerator over too many days, but she will not compromise on price over taste and nutrition.

Tracey Kennedy, a young professional mother, wants her son to learn healthy eating habits and to be exposed to many different types of foods, more than the three different kinds of canned vegetables she ate growing up. She tries to buy a variety of vegetables and lower fat protein ("I can't go to the co-op and buy grass-fed beef because we can't afford it, but at least I can get ninety percent lean") and tries to avoid sweeteners:

I try to buy foods with natural sugar, like dried fruit or trail mix . . . I feel like it's meeting that pyramid guide for some level of a fruit whereas those fruit gummy things they have for kids don't fill that bill.

Other shoppers explicitly seek out information on nutrition and read articles and books on the alternative discourses about nutrition. They discuss eating organic and pesticide-free foods and they emphasize local foods. Those with time and money can translate this knowledge into action and employ a variety of different food provisioning strategies including growing food, visiting farmers' markets, buying from bakeries, and visiting local farms.

Colin Moore said he usually doesn't think about health concerns when purchasing food but acknowledged that his wife does. "Meg thinks more about buying organic food; for instance, over time she is getting organic carrots instead of the regular ones." Meg corroborated his response with this story. She signed up for a Community Supported Agriculture (CSA) subscription in order to get organic food for her family. It was difficult for her to justify the price and when her husband found out he was somewhat shocked. "If I'm without him and I'm shopping I feel more freedom to buy stuff that's more expensive because he just gets more edgy about it." He does support what she is doing but is not as concerned about healthy food. Meg stated that "Colin thinks about food a lot but not in the same way. It's not so much we need to buy local or we need to buy organic, it's like just different methods of cooking or different things to do that he hasn't thought of before."

Meg was reading more about the nutritional value of the food her family ate as well as the larger state of the food system. After she became pregnant a second time, she began questioning the larger food system:

Food travels thousands of miles to get to the dinner table—not sustainable at all! And it makes no sense. Yet I just bought squash at my local grocery store that came from Michigan when I know full well that there is local squash at the farmers' market—which I never have time to go to because they have such limited hours. That made me feel bad, knowing I was participating in a destructive system.

So she searched on the Internet for local grains, cheese, and vegetable growers and found herself going to many different stores, including the supermarket for nonlocal foods, the farmers' market on Saturdays, the local co-op, and several local farms for fresh produce. After she went back to work, this type of shopping abruptly stopped. She stated:

> I stopped feeling guilty about buying produce at the grocery store when I realized that it is NOT possible. Supporting sustainable agriculture is not sustainable in our society. Now I still get my few things at the local health food store but just get the rest from the supermarket. I bake quick breads every other week, but not bread-bread. I just don't have the time. I feel like I don't have much of a choice anymore but to just participate in the system. It basically sucks.

Many middle-class professional mothers like Meg want their kids to eat more local or organic food but find it is too labor intensive to shop for organic or local groceries and produce. Jessica Pierce expressed significant anxiety over the pesticides in the food that her kids eat and believes conventional food to be "chock-full" of hormones and pesticides. She expressed guilt over not putting more time into food shopping but she found that organic food costs significantly more and she doesn't have time to cook from scratch. The farmers' market, for instance, is open only twice a week during her work hours. But as her work can last until eight on some nights, many times she is just focused on getting her kids fed before they go to bed, and sometimes cannot count on her husband to help her:

> One time when I got home at nine, my five-year-old son said that he was hungry. When I asked him what he had for dinner he said "nothing." My husband said, "Oh yeah, I forgot to feed them." I don't worry so much about my eleven-year-old daughter who can fend for herself, maybe find a frozen microwaveable dish in the freezer and heat it up, but my five-year-old can't.

CONCLUSION

All shoppers have to contend with a nutrition discourse that relies on reducing and quantifying food to scientific properties. Although there are alternative discourses, such as the slow food and local food movements, most Americans are aware of the mainstream nutrition discourse and many organizations such as supermarkets, school lunch programs, and so forth incorporate these dictates. The federal government creates and promotes this discourse through several different agencies, including the Departments of Agriculture,

Health and Human Services, and the Food and Drug Administration, which is disseminated by dieticians, healthcare providers through schools, agencies, and media outlets.

This information is not only available, but is reinforced by other institutional agents. The school that Meg Moore's daughter attends asks that each parent fill out a health grade card every week. Meg has to calculate how many fruits and vegetables her child ate each day and how many minutes of exercise she got. If the parent fills out the card each week, the child will get a prize at the end of the month—a little shoelace ornament. Kids then collect these as they go through the year and Meg stated that she feels a lot of pressure to turn in the card because her child is embarrassed if she doesn't have as many orna-ments on her shoes as her classmates. Meg also feels inadequate when she is filling out the cards because her child rarely gets five servings a day of fruits and vegetables, even though she feels that they eat healthy.

Most shoppers with children express some level of responsibility for the nutrition in the food they purchase for their children. While working-class women express some knowledge of the nutrition discourse, they give little credence to its dictates, perhaps due to distrust of authorities in general, but also because they have to contend with how to feed their families on a limited budget. Fresh fruits and vegetables are expensive and in the rural store they are either not readily available or are of low quality. Middle-class women, es-pecially professionals, are very familiar with this discourse but in keeping with the culture of intensive mothering (Hays 1996), tend to spend a great deal of emotional and physical labor trying to live up to its standards. This raises the level of anxiety in their work of food provisioning.

The discourses discussed in the next chapters, the efficiency discourse and the food industry discourse, expose shoppers to additional layers of in-formation and messages that often conflict with each other and often make it more difficult for women to provision households.

–4–

The Efficient Housewife Discourse

In the previous two chapters we've seen that food shopping involves performing physical labor, negotiating household relationships, and understanding messages from a nutrition discourse that make providing healthy food an individual responsibility. This chapter will focus on another aspect of food shopping: shopping as a process of household management. Food purchases comprise 6–10 percent of the average household expenditure depending on income level (U.S. Department of Labor 2007a), which is a historically and globally low amount to spend on food per household. When I asked shoppers about budgeting and how much money they usually spend on food, only two could give me an exact amount. Two-thirds of the shoppers I interviewed, from a wide income range, said they spent $100 a week. This seeming discrepancy can partially be explained by the routine nature of most shopping trips because most shoppers tend to get roughly the same items every week or have a set of basics that they know they need to have on hand and thus spend about the same amount every week whether or not they are aware of the amount.

But what explains the widespread focus on saving money as a bedrock principle of grocery shopping? Jackie Engle starts her food shopping when the ads come in the Wednesday mail. She has a mental idea of what kind of food her family will eat and plans out the weekly menu by what is on sale. She writes the list according to the store layout ("in case someone else will be shopping," she laughs), meaning she lists grocery items starting with produce, then dairy, meats, and grocery items by aisle. She explained her planning rationale like this:

> If I were in the store every day I would spend thirty dollars. That would be $900 a month! It's worth your time to do your menu, buy everything you need, and I don't care if you had to invest six hours doing it—if you made a weekly menu and knew exactly the stuff you needed—you would spend less because you wouldn't be at the store all the time. And we all tend to go when we're hungry when we spend more.

Kay Worthington also plans her meals around the Wednesday sale ads. When the ads come in the mail, she takes out her large leather planner and plans her meals around what is on sale. She tries to have several menu ideas for certain days but then leaves open other days thinking she can either serve leftovers on that day or if she has some extra time she may run by the grocery store. Writing her list on a notepad in her planner, she flips through the ads several times to make sure she has not missed anything. She showed me her most recent list: asparagus, spiral ham, pineapple, Barilla pasta, and tuna. She explained that those items were on sale that week and she planned to make meals from those items, but she would never buy food that her family would not normally eat since they may not like it.

She feels like she is being an economical shopper this way and would "just die if I bought something and later it was on sale. I would feel like a failure,

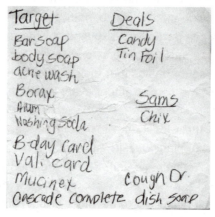

Figure 4.1   Grocery lists from shoppers.

like I should have known better and bought it when it was on sale because it is the right thing to do." She feels that she is helping with the family bills by reducing the household grocery costs.

Stacey Ostrander told me a story about her husband and junk food. He once went to the store and bought potato chips at the regular price, something that Stacey just couldn't live with. She said:

> Gary is the snack food person, and I've tried weaning him off snack foods. I didn't buy any and I let it run out. But that didn't work because when I buy them I buy them on sale three for five dollars. Well, when we ran out, he just went to the store and paid full price! It's like you just paid $3.45; I paid $1.60. We have carrots in the house, we have bananas in the house, there are grapes in the house, there are apples in the house. There is always fresh fruit and veggies in my house. Eat something healthy! So I gave up and just started buying it again because I can save money that way. You feel funny when you are walking out with six bags of junk food, but if it's on sale for three for five dollars and you are going to eat it (*sic*).

Spending time to save money, being an economical shopper—shoppers indicated that they are being good shoppers when they save money at the grocery store. Sue and Kay indirectly articulated that their work preparing for shopping is the "other side of the paycheck" (cf. Weinbaum and Bridges 1976); in other words, they contribute to the household budget and supplement their spouses' and their own wages by shopping efficiently.

In the twenty interviews I did with household food providers, I heard many shopping strategies: plan meals in advance, always shop with a list, buy on sale, shop at night without kids, don't allow husbands to shop alone. Everyone knows that making a list contributes to saving money and time in that it keeps the shopper focused on buying only products that are needed and shortens the time spent in the store.

But on what advice are these shoppers basing their strategies? What does being a good shopper mean? Where do shoppers get their information about shopping strategies? In analyzing the texts shoppers use, I identified a discourse I call "the efficient housewife" or efficiency discourse for short. The efficiency discourse has historical roots in the home economics movement (see discussion in Chapter 2), is contemporarily administered by federal institutions such as the USDA and its extension services, and has filtered into

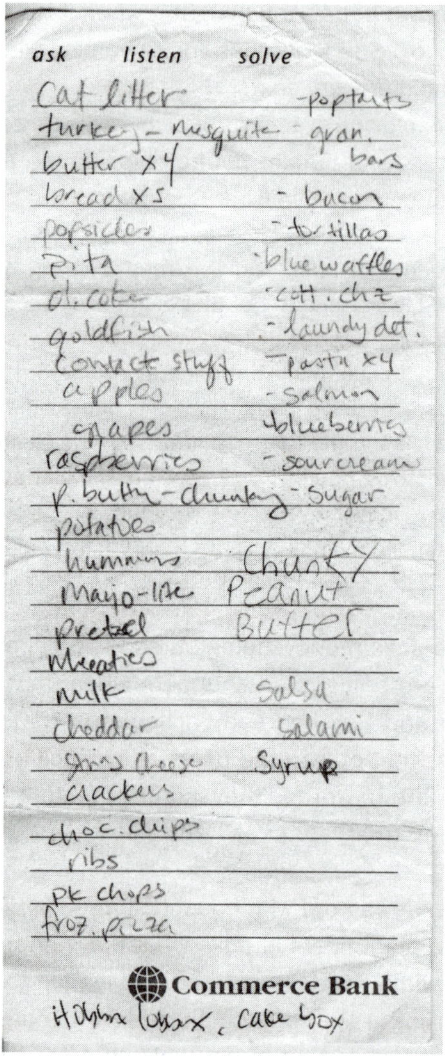

Figure 4.2   Grocery lists from shoppers.

media outlets such as television news shows, the Internet, and women's magazines. There is a contradiction between the ubiquitousness of this discourse and the demographic changes in household composition because it still assumes a housewife is available to manage the household. I will lay out the main tenets of this discourse and then discuss how it structures shoppers' work.

EFFICIENT HOUSEWIFE DISCOURSE

The efficient food consumer is one who plans meals out in advance of the actual shopping trip, creates a list of products based on these meal plans, makes sure she is getting the best deal for her money, avoids buying things she doesn't need, uses coupons, and shops the sales. The experts who write and produce stories about this discourse include nutritionists, dieticians, extension officers, financial advisors, and corporate representatives, among others. One of the main themes of this discourse is that the efficient house-wife should be organized, disciplined to withstand impulse buys, stay within the budget, and make rational choices.

PRE-SHOPPING STRATEGIES

Planning meals for the week is the first step in the process of being an efficient shopper. Stephanie Nelson, the "coupon mom" and ABC correspondent, advises:

> Plan meals for the week before you make your shopping list. Make sure you have the basics on hand to create a week's worth of meals. Write the meals planned on a piece of paper and post it on the refrigerator to remember. (Nelson 2007a)

The United States Department of Health and Human Services advises shoppers to "Think ahead about the meals you plan to make and write a list of what you'll need to buy" (U.S. Department of Health and Human Services 2006). The Academy of Nutrition and Dietetics, at the time known as American Dietetic Association, reminds the shopper when making a list to keep in mind "which days you will have time to cook from scratch and which days you will be pressed for time to put dinner on the table. Organize the list, checking menu options against the food guide pyramid" (American Dietetic Association 2003).

Experts also advise shoppers to write the list to correspond to the aisles in which the store is set out. Phil Lempert, the self-proclaimed "supermarket guru" and NBC *Today Show* correspondent describes his suggested list:

> [U]se your old receipts and cross off all the items you didn't need. Then look in your refrigerator, cupboards and freezer to see what you are missing, and add these products to the list. 2) Write any additional items that you will need in the

aisle order. 3) Under the additional items draw a horizontal line for each of your "allowed" impulse items. Keep the number of impulse items fixed from week to week—don't vary it. That wastes time and money. (Lempert 2007a)

An article on organizing from *Real Simple*, a middle-class women's magazine, adds several steps to the list-making process:

> Make a list, grouped by aisles. Add all items you stock your shelves with that you don't need to buy this time. Take this list to the store. As you shop, write down the aisle number next to each item on the list. When you get home, type up the list according to the aisle numbers. Print several copies and stick on the refrigerator. Superglue mini magnets to a pen and a small stapler and keep both on fridge next to your list. When you run out of an item, use the pen to check it off. Staple coupons to the list and write C next to items for "double insurance." (Humphreys 2004)

The main reason for the list is to keep the shopper from buying any items or products she does not need, or in other words, "impulse items." The list also keeps the shopper on task and in the store the least amount of time as possible, and thus away from temptation. The shopping list should not only save you money but also help you avoid buying items you don't need. According to Kansas State Extension Service professionals, the average shopper spends 40 percent more on impulse purchases when shopping without a list (Henry and Higgins 2006).

Efficient housewives also favor thriftiness over convenience. Shoppers should cook and bake more from scratch in order to save money on convenience foods. For example, instead of frozen chicken breasts, the shopper should buy a whole chicken and cut it into pieces (U.S. Department of Health and Human Services 2005b). The "Shopping on a Shoestring" author extends this advice to suggest we learn how to butcher and use all the parts of a chicken as the first steps to real economy in the kitchen (Friedman 2007). Shoppers should also do batch cooking and freeze some for future meals, as well as "assemble healthy snacks at home in small baggies" rather than buying prepackaged snacks (American Dietetic Association 2003). *Consumer Reports* tells shoppers to "shred it yourself and save: a 1 pound bag of Dole whole carrots in New York cost 99 cents while a 10-ounce bag of Dole shredded carrots costs $1.99" ("Win at the Grocery Game" 2006). Shoppers should avoid convenience foods, which are of course more expensive. For example, since individual packets of oatmeal are more expensive, the shopper should buy a large container and add fruit ("Meal Planning and Shopping" 2006).

Your meals are planned; your list is made. What other strategies will save money? The advice on coupon use is mixed. Coupons, when used for products you need or regularly buy, can definitely save money. *Consumer Reports* states that coupons save $30 billion a year. However, coupons can also entice you to buy products you may not need or that may be unhealthy. Shoppers are thus encouraged to be judicious in their use of coupons.

But if you were to use coupons correctly, you may be able to whittle your food bill to nothing. The "coupon mom," Stephanie Nelson, has written an entire book dedicated to shopping with coupons. Many of her advanced saving strategies involve a detailed understanding of retail coupon policies as well as retrieving and managing coupons once you get them. She states that she saves more than fifty dollars a week with coupons, as well as fifty dollars a week just on sale prices. This management system takes time to organize, however. She suggests using the Virtual Coupon Organizer, an interactive database listing all the grocery coupons that have come out in the newspaper. To use this site:

> Create a "best grocery deals" list for an unlisted store and sort the list alphabetically to create your own best deals. When you see an item you need on sale, you can quickly see if a grocery coupon is available for the item. Check the boxes to display your list. Once you have your printed list of coupons needed at your store, you can sit down with your collection of saved circulars and cut out only the coupons needed. Sort the list by expiration date, to make sure you take advantage of coupons that will be expiring soon. (Nelson 2007b)

The "coupon mom" prefigured a couponing craze. Television shows like *Extreme Couponing* now highlight consumers' ability (and compulsion) to clip coupons for pennies on the dollar to buy products they might not even need. Ordinary shoppers can sign up for daily e-mails that feature manufacturers' and retail coupons, although many still comb through the Wednesday and Sunday newspaper ads to get better deals. There is even a coupon app for phones that allows customers to download coupons at the store. But again, the shoppers only save money if they only buy what they need.

In addition to coupons, shoppers should go to more than one store for the best buys. A *Women's Day* article states that:

[S]hoppers who hit two stores in one day saved $15 on average, compared to those who shopped in only one store. Make it a habit to shop at another store besides your favorite supermarket, and that's close to 800 dollars in savings a year. Go first to one or two bargain stores, then buy whatever else you need from your primary grocery store. Buy as many items as possible in bulk at shopping clubs. (Steele 2007)

Another important strategy in resisting temptation and being efficient is to leave the kids at home. According to the experts, grocery shopping with children can add $100 to $400 to your grocery bill (Steele 2007). Stephanie Nelson advises shoppers to leave the kids at home if possible to avoid *their* impulse purchases. But if you can't, you should set up a reward system like a fun activity or a free cookie at the bakery if they don't ask for anything (Nelson 2007b). Other experts suggest shoppers should go to the store when the kids are busy because shopping is faster if you go alone. "Plan grocery store forays when the kids are at school or music lessons, or have your spouse mind them while you shop" (Weinstein and Scarbrough 2007). If you have to take your kids, have something for them to do, perhaps a game or a way they can practice shopping. A *Women's Day* article gives this advice:

Train little shoppers. Grocery shopping with children can add 100–400 dollars a month to your bill. With kids you spend more time in the store but also kids are masters of impulse buying. If you can't go solo, turn the kids into smart shoppers. Give them choices or have them use real money for anything not on the list. (Steele 2007)

The Academy of Nutrition and Dietetics advises that "an enjoyable grocery shopping experience with children is possible! Use it as an opportunity to give your kids a lesson in color, smell, and names of new foods. Engaging them in the food selection can turn a trip to the store into a great teaching tool about nutritious food choices" (American Dietetic Association 2003).

The last issue to consider before you enter the store is your mood. One of the most universal recommendations is to make preparations to be in the right frame of mind before shopping. Avoiding temptation in the face of the myriad choices in the marketplace is a central theme throughout this discourse. Shoppers should make sure to eat before going grocery shopping so they are less tempted to buy too much or the wrong kind of food. Shoppers should not be stressed out either; the expert shopper is always on guard to resist supermarket strategies. "Everything about the supermarket is designed to prolong your trip" ("Win at the Grocery Game" 2006).

The "supermarket guru" Phil Lempert (2007a) advises shoppers:

Never shop when you're hungry. You'll end up with all kinds of impulse items in your cart. Another rule is not to shop when you're stressed out. The crowds and lines will only make you more frustrated. Some people, however, find the supermarket to be therapeutic. Figure out which type of shopper you are, and shop when it suits your mood.

A Weight Watchers article advises shoppers:

Shop on a full stomach. If you shop when you are hungry, you're subject to spur-of-the-moment cravings and impulse buys. To manage the lifestyle you want, shop after lunch or dinner. (Weinstein and Scarbrough 2007)

Christine Palumbo, a registered dietician, states that "when you are hungry, everything looks good so don't go hungry. Likewise if you are frazzled or feeling down, save the trip for later when you are less vulnerable to impulse buys" (Hennen 2006). An article in *Health* advises shoppers to "make sure you've eaten and go shopping when you are in a calm, stable mood. Hunger and stress make you more susceptible to temptation" (Haspel 2006).

Shoppers should also make plans to shop on the same day every week and at times when few shoppers will be in the same store. One dietician advises shoppers to "[S]hop on the same day if possible and spare yourself aggravation by avoiding the busy times: weekday evenings or weekends" (Jibrin 2007). One of the worst times to shop in terms of crowds, under-stocked shelves, and overworked employees is weekdays between 4:00 p.m. and 7:00 p.m.; one of the best times for highest efficiency is early Friday afternoon, before the weekend rush but after the store is stocked ("How to Make the Most of Grocery Shopping" 2008).

IN-STORE STRATEGIES

After all the planning is done, the kids are at the sitter's, and the shopper has eaten a light and healthy snack, what are the most efficient ways to shop once in the store? Most experts advise the shopper to stay on the perimeter of the store. The produce, bakery, meat, and dairy aisles provide the healthiest and freshest foods. Try to avoid the big outside aisle, known as "the race track," where the shopper is encouraged to browse good sales or delicacies like imported cheeses (Gibbons 2007). *Consumer Reports* even advises shoppers to ignore the standard store setup and shop clockwise, which encourages the shopper to spend less time in the store and therefore save more money ("Win at the Grocery Game" 2006).

Shoppers should be aware of the strategies managers use to encourage purchases. Managers stock their most expensive brands or their private labels at eye level, so shoppers should look at the highest and lowest shelves for generics and specials, and buy store brands or generics that are often placed higher or lower on the grocery store shelves (U.S. Department of Health and Human Services 2005a). "Buy one, get one free" sounds good, but often the "one" is marked up to begin with. Managers will also use "loss leaders" such as a brand name cereal that they are willing to sell at cost or less to attract customers who will buy other products while in the store, so shoppers should be wary of shopping at a store for a certain sale ("Win at the Grocery Game" 2006).

The shopper should read and compare labels. Unit prices are displayed on the store shelves below the foods and shoppers should use these to compare the cost on different-sized packages ("Meal Planning and Shopping" 2006). Some experts advise to buy in bulk (Kramer 2008), but sometimes bigger packages may not be more economical. The shopper should then use unit prices to make a decision, especially when one size is on sale ("Win at the Grocery Game" 2006). Shoppers should also compare prices in different parts of the same store. Sometimes cheese, for instance, is more expensive in the deli than in the dairy case. Shoppers should also think about buying seasonal and local to save money on the shipping (Friedman 2007). If you can't get fresh produce, frozen fruits and vegetables are fine, including peas, broccoli, corn kernels, and berries (weightwatchers.com).

NOTES FROM REAL LIFE

Making lists, checking receipts, cutting coupons, shopping sales—all these strategies take time and planning. The efficiency discourse assumes a household with a housewife, someone who has this time and inclination to assume the role of efficient purchaser. This discourse is especially relevant for households where saving money is important. In my study this discourse was more salient for women who were not working for wages outside the home, who were working part time, or who had only one wage earner in the household. The work of provisioning is approached differently depending on employment status. For example, using ads is rarely a concern for full-time workers. In fact, none of the working mothers I interviewed used the Wednesday ads regularly, if at all. April Malloy, a full-time worker who spends much of her time commuting, summed it up: "I used to do all that: cut coupons, look at the ads. I used to spend a hundred bucks a month on food. I would go to Food 4 Less and I would get all these things and that's when I used to stockpile when the kids were babies. I was very efficient." What asked what changed, she replied:

> Time. I don't have the time to go through and look at all the prices and try to find the best deals and spend the time looking for all that. I think it's just the time factor—I've got fifteen minutes and I need to pick up supper and I've got to zoom through here . . . I just don't want to spend my time doing that. I need to be on the road doing other things like taking the girls to ball and tumbling.

Jessica Pierce, another working mom, stated:

> I don't use coupons or ads because that would require me to go to several stores and have a lot more time devoted to that than probably what we would devote to it, or than I would like to devote to it. I mean, if something is on sale and it's something I want I would consider myself lucky that night, I suppose.

So there is a tradeoff between time and money. The mothers who work for wages have the luxury of spending money on full-priced items (and not spending time cutting coupons or comparison shopping), but are squeezed for time in terms of shopping and preparing the meal. Maggie Waggoner loves to shop and cook, but when she gets off work at 5:30 p.m. and needs to have meals on the table at 6:00 p.m., she does not have the luxury of spending much time in the grocery store. In terms of making dinner, she will "either go home and look around thinking, 'What do I have on hand?' or think about what can I quick stop and get on my way home? I'm not near as organized about it as I used to be when I wasn't working as much."

For some working mothers, the organization and planning of shopping takes on a larger role the more hours they work outside the home. Two mothers in the study had just experienced transitions from working part time to working full time. They found that they had to be more efficient in order to get both the wage work and the shopping work done and spent considerable time on the weekends planning meals for the week, as well as creating lists and planning when they could actually do the shopping. Their shopping was much more leisurely when they had more time to devote to it.

Eating out was a more frequent strategy for full-time wage workers, and more than one working mom assuaged her guilt of eating out by taking her kids to Subway instead of McDonalds. But I surmise that eating out was also underreported. When asked how many times they would eat out, shoppers would state not very often; when asked for specific meals they had made over the course of a week, many would report eating out at least once a week, if not more. Although I didn't probe at the time, I believe that eating out still carries a stigma of not being a good food provisioner.

Almost all part-time workers reported knowing and using some form of the efficiency discourse. Karen Calhoun stated that "I go through the ad and look for the things we normally use, anything that's on sale that I might want or that sounds good, I open up the pantry, open up the cabinets, OK, what are we low on, and make my list from there." She does report that she is constantly tempted by things that are not on her list or that look good in the store, even if they are pricey. However, she always stocks up on products that her family will use if they are on sale. For instance, during her last grocery visit, Best Choice Vegetables were on sale for twenty-nine cents, and she bought the maximum number allowed.

Melissa Long, whose children are now out of the house, remembered how she used to shop when her four kids were young: "With the kids, I actually looked at ads and made lists. And when I was a stay-at-home mom I went once a week in Lawrence so I had my whole menus for the week planned out and what I needed and I just shopped that way and of course we raised so much of our own food at that time." She used to look at the ads and compare what was on sale. She used to cut coupons and made a detailed list. Now, with just her and her husband at home and with her full-time salary, she shops whenever she wants or is out of something. She states: "I very seldom shop like I used to. I'm one of those, if it's frozen and it microwaves real good, I know. You know how I do my cinnamon rolls [she uses Rhodes rather than make them from scratch]. I think it's because of the way I work. You know, when I get home at night, I'm tired, and Harry's tired and hungry, and I need something that cooks fast and quickly and a lot of times our suppers consist of some type of meat, vegetables, and a salad."

Many part-time wage workers could list prices from memory. Jane Smith remembered that Tide with Downey is $6.47 for 100 oz. at Walmart; if the local store is selling it cheaper she will pick up a bottle or two. Even though she is not fond of Walmart, she stated, "You just can't beat the price." Another shopper, Jackie Engle, who also uses price as a main factor in her decision-making process, stated that chicken tenders at Aldi's are $6.89, whereas they are $8.99 at the local store. Karen Calhoun knew that the price of milk is twenty cents higher at the local store than at one of the discount grocery stores.

But some shoppers don't have the same orientation to price and/or efficiency which leads to consequences for their family's provisioning. Kelly Barnes, a single mother of three school-aged children, described her shopping preparation:

> I don't put much thought into it, I really don't. I don't make menus, I don't make lists; I just think about what we need. It's very rare that I don't have to go to the store two, three, four times during the week. Honestly that's because we just kind of get through a day or two . . . I just kind of fly by the seat of my pants.

She recognized that if she were more organized, she could save herself money and buy better food to eat.

> As a single mom who does struggle from paycheck to paycheck, should I be on a budget, should I look at ads and all that sort of thing? It makes sense. Yes, I probably should. But I just don't have the time or inclination. I just really don't have a budget for anything. I just pay what I can pay, I mean, seriously. I mean, usually I can make it from paycheck to paycheck and most of the time I'm sweating by the end and that's just the way it is. I'm really bad about that. I know if I was a better budgeter or if I spent my money better that I wouldn't be sweating at the end of the month, but if I'm going to eat it I want it to taste good.

Kelly's kids are getting old enough that they can walk to the store to get some ingredients and cook basic meals like spaghetti. But usually their schedule is so busy they end up eating sandwiches, or some kind of frozen dinner, or something from the school concession stand.

> Sometimes I get home at 4:15 or 4:30; sometimes I don't get home until 5:00 or 5:30, so that just depends. There is extracurricular stuff a lot of times too, so if I get to come home and just get to worry about dinner, then that is one thing,

but usually there is other stuff going on. Like every day this week we have other stuff going on, there's no time. I'm even thinking, OK, taco salad may wait until next week because if we are out and it is late, its 7:00, 7:30, or 8:00 when we get home. I don't cook dinner. And usually the girls are getting ready for bed or finishing up homework and taking showers. I mean we just need to eat and move on.

She felt guilty about not cooking—"I think I'm supposed to cook for my kids because I am the mom"—but she just doesn't have the time and when she gets home from work and coaching, she is so tired she just wants to sit down and relax:

> And I feel guilty and especially after teaching junior high I don't like what I do and it's stressful every single day. Sometimes it's more stressful and then I come home and the kids are fighting and doing whatever and sometimes I think to myself, "I don't want to eat with you guys, I just want to be by myself." And I do feel guilty about that. And especially because Maggie will say, "Eat at the table, Mom."

Kelly recognized that if she were more organized, if she spent more time planning menus and clipping coupons, she could save money and not live paycheck to paycheck. But she also has very little discretionary time to plan after working a full day and then caring for three children. She also values eating what tastes good to her, not what is "on sale," which is what she is supposed to buy under the tenets of the efficient housewife discourse. She is not willing to deny herself what tastes good to her to buy a cheaper substitute even though she cannot afford it. One small example she gave was her taco sauce, Spanish Gardens, a more expensive brand that she has always eaten and that tastes better than cheaper sauces.

Peggy Fiske does not have the luxury of ignoring the efficiency strategies; her household's survival depends on her success at being an effective shopper. She receives $363 a month from food stamps to feed herself and her two children. She is proud that she can feed her family on this amount and her strategies include using coupons, store discount cards, making a list, and finding the best sales when she is at the store. She can't really stock up on these sales since her freezer is very small and she doesn't have extra space in her small apartment. She can't afford a newspaper subscription so she doesn't get the larger store's advertisements to plan from. She does, however, take a calculator with her and adds up her purchases as she goes along. If she forgets a calculator, she says "sometimes I'll just sit there and

I'll write everything up and I'll keep track on like the side of my list how much I've spent."

She does spend money on packaged foods like Hamburger Helper (which she doctors with extra seasoning) and the Homestyle Bakes with everything in the kit because it makes it so much easier for her to cook with two small children in the house: "The quick stuff comes in very handy and there are times when I am just exhausted and I don't feel up to making a big meal but I have to cook something." They rarely eat out, because it is too expensive and it is difficult to maneuver her son's wheelchair in a restaurant. If they eat out, it is fast food, perhaps Taco Bell, where they can get "filled up" for a reasonable amount of money.

She tries to look for sales on rice and other staples that she can use to "stretch" foods, but sometimes her older son will eat one meal really well and refuse to eat it another time. She coordinates meals not only so she will not waste any food but also so the kids won't get tired of eating the same things repeatedly:

> One night I'll make a roast and then . . . sometimes it's beef, sometimes it's pork; depends on what looked good or what was on sale. And then the next night I'll make pork and noodles or I'll make beef and noodles, and I use the broth that I've got from baking the roast because my broth always comes out really, really rich and just so much better than if you'd get a can of broth to cook your meals in. And I've used the broth and sometimes I'll make mashed potatoes I will eat until my stomach hurts. And you know it's a way to get the stuff used up but the kids don't realize so much that they are having leftovers.

Peggy was thrifty enough to manage the small amount of money she receives and feed her family. She also receives assistance through the free/reduced school lunch program, as well as private programs such as Kid Screen. Families receiving food stamps also receive monitoring on whether they are using these programs effectively, and if not will often be referred to agencies such as the USDA's Expanded Food and Nutrition Education Program (EFNEP). This agency provides food resource management training to identified families and posts success stories on its website, stories of shoppers who successfully incorporated the efficient housewife strategies in their work of grocery shopping.

The underlying theme is that by teaching efficiency skills, the household not only is better off, but manages the state's money more effectively. One success story is Sue in Iowa. She never had any money left over at the end of the month, and the EFNEP nutrition assistant worked with Sue for three months to set a budget and plan for grocery shopping. Sue now can keep track of her income and expenses; she plans her meals two weeks in advance and shops according to a grocery list. She is also catching up on other bills (Cooperative State Research, Education and Extension Service 2006). Another mother in Illinois learned how to plan weekly meals by constructing a weekly budget and getting the newspaper to check for sales and coupons. "The success the mother got from improving her diet gave her the security she needed to improve the rest of her life. She now has a settled living arrangement and is exploring her job prospects" (Cooperative State Research, Education and Extension Service 2006).

These mothers have made the successful transition to efficient consumer, but we do not see all the work involved in the process. A local newspaper food editor, Jill Wendholt Silva, took the Food Stamp Challenge and attempted to feed her family on $129.50 per week, which is the maximum amount a family of four can receive on food stamps. What strategies did she utilize to make sure she could feed her family? Her approach read right from the efficiency discourse: make a menu for the week, check the weekly food ads, make a shopping list and stick to it, be a "smart shopper" by comparing prices, know the store layout, and shop at more than one store. However, it is her reaction to this experience that is instructive. She wrote:

> I spent nearly every moment I was not at work thinking about or preparing food. I constantly feared I would run out of food. It was exhausting to shop three times in one week to get the best deals. Even though I stayed on a budget, our entire family lost the freedom to choose what to eat and when. (Silva 2007)

She was also skeptical that anyone who worked a full-time job could actually pull off this kind of planning week after week.

Retailers and grocery stores benefit from shoppers adopting efficient food shopping strategies. Contrary to conventional wisdom about higher profits on convenience foods, the retailers I spoke with reported that an efficient consumer is more profitable for their stores. For example, marketing research indicates that customers whose main shopping goals are to care for their families, shop efficiently, and use smart budgeting strategies account for almost half of all supermarket trips and almost 63 percent of total supermarket spending (Coca-Cola Retailing Research Council of North America 2008). With the rise in fast foods and restaurants, grocery stores and supermarkets must

contend with competition from already prepared food and takeout from restaurants. Making a meal from scratch to eat at home usually costs more than
buying a prepared meal, and consumers who make meals at home are usually
more loyal customers. One corporate sales manager explained:

> Great shoppers make a list and they come to the store prepared. They're great
> shoppers in the fact that they're organized and they still eat at home, you know
> that is not always the case anymore. There's a lot of people that fly by the seat
> of their pants, they run in the store, they don't plan anything, they run in the store
> every day, they are good shoppers too . . . Mrs. Brown who makes a list and
> comes once a week usually has a nice big order one time. We know that she is
> a regular customer and everybody else kind of flies by the seat of their pants. Al-
> though they might be regular customers, but they might be just as apt to pull into
> Hy-Vee because they are over there and getting something from them. Usually I
> think there are people that lay out all of the ads and go to all the stores because
> they have nothing else to do but that is a dying breed. So we like the people that
> still have family dinner and still eat at home.

CONCLUSION

What we hear in the shoppers' descriptions of their work is a certain kind of
knowledge about how to get food from the store shelves into their homes that
derives from the emphasis on efficiency that prevails in our modern economic
system. How and why do we learn that getting a bargain or shopping the
sale means being a good shopper or provisioner? Learning and remembering
prices, comparison shopping, clipping coupons—all of these activities take
time and involve certain knowledge based not so much on the needs of the
family but based on the dictates of the political economy of the food system.
A certain kind of rationality is necessary for being a successful food shopper,
a rationality of efficiency.

While being an efficient shopper may save time in the grocery store, it
does not necessarily mean less work for shoppers. The efficiency discourse
instructs the shopper not only to save money but to discipline herself against
the onslaught of choices at the supermarket. The shopper must spend time
making lists and meal plans, comparison shopping, checking the ads, and
arranging child care. In the store, the shopper must fight her impulse to buy
the wrong product or too much of a product; she must exhibit self-discipline

to balance economy with nutrition. In this way she will save her household money, stretch the wage dollars that come in, and allow for the purchase of other consumer goods.

Full-time, wage-earning shoppers from two-earner households who participated in my study were aware of the efficiency discourse but were less likely to follow these strategies because of time constraints and the ability to pay for food and services. Working-class shoppers and part-time workers usually were trying to save money through shopping and used the efficiency strategies such as planning meals, comparison shopping, and so forth, which took extra time to accomplish and became part of their job of saving money for the household. For households that do not fit the "standard North American family" paradigm, such as single-parent households, buying food on one income often without the luxury of time is a real feat. In fact, if these shoppers did not use some of these efficiency strategies they probably would not be able to make ends meet. However, when all shoppers enter the store they are confronted with another set of challenges: navigating a retail environment designed to get them to buy more. This is the story of the next chapter.

The contradiction between the efficient housewife discourse and the experiences of real-life shoppers is especially sharp for those shoppers who do not fit the necessary structural characteristics of the housewife, especially having the luxury of time or money to fulfill the efficiency tenets. The two single mothers in my study had the most difficult time managing both time and money. Managing jobs, money, and children (in one case a disabled child) was a balancing act that involved many strategies including shopping at low-price stores like Walmart, using federal subsidies and child support payments, and even alternative financial strategies such as floating checks. Acker (2006) argues that this structural reality for some women reflects the class structure in the United States, defining class broader than income, education, and status to include "unequal power and control over, and access to, the means of provisioning . . . this disadvantage is most evident in the case of those who have low-paying jobs or who have no family [husbands] to provide money" (Acker 2006).

Larger social institutions in the complex of the relations of ruling have a significant interest in the consumer becoming a successful household manager. Grocery shopping is a specific form of economic activity that is crucial not only to the household's survival strategy but also for the functioning of larger social institutions. Economists are now worried that higher food prices will mean less money spent on discretionary items like clothes and entertainment, those goods and services that have driven the consumer society since the end of World War II. Keeping the grocery dollar to a minimum means more dollars circulating elsewhere.

Not only does the economy in general depend on consumer spending, but other social institutions have a stake in how households spend their food dollars. The federal government, through agencies like the USDA and the HHS, is concerned not only with providing information on food and nutrition but also educating shoppers on how to be efficient with their money, since many of the shoppers they are educating are on federal subsidies such as SNAP (Supplemental Assistance Program), TANF (Temporary Assistance to Needy Families), and WIC (Women, Infants and Children). An inefficient shopper not only deprives her family of food, but also costs taxpayers money.

Finally, efficient shoppers also spend more money in the grocery store. Managers indicate that efficient shoppers are better for the store's bottom line because they buy more at one time, are more likely to shop at one store, and are more likely to eat meals at home rather than restaurants (their main competition). However, while managers and store owners prefer good shoppers, the retail discourse discussed in the next chapter instructs them in practices to encourage particular buying habits, including impulse shopping and buying new products.

The Consumer Control Discourse

Cal Dipman, an industry advertiser in the 1930s, looked into the future and foresaw a time when the supermarket not only sold products but also had spaces like a customers' rest corner for people to relax. "It should be a friendly spot," he wrote, "a grouping of tables, comfortable, colorful chairs, and if possible a telephone, fern stand, lamp, pads and pencils, a magazine or two. This is a good spot, too, for a radio or a canary, if the store has them. The rest corner should be located where customers can observe store activity, for people like to watch others work or play" (Dipman 1931: 148–49, quoted in Bowlby 1997).

While the supermarket today is often more like a warehouse than the home-like setting envisioned by Dipman, the physical environment of the grocery store can have a profound effect on the labor necessary to shop for food. The design of the store, aisle and product placement, sales and promotions, and signage significantly shape shoppers' experience. As we saw in Chapter 2, the supermarket is a retail organization that relies on marketing and advertising to encourage shoppers to buy increasingly standardized products. Managers and owners are central to this strategy, and their work is also shaped by extra-local discourses that operate to support the supermarket strategy.

In order to explore the management of the supermarket, which is the next level in our investigation of grocery shopping as an institution, I interviewed seven managers (the names listed are pseudonyms): Chris Morris, the head manager of a no-frills suburban store; Craig Wallace, the assistant manager at a full-service suburban store; Frank O'Donnell, the owner and manager of a rural store; and Mike Stephens, a sales manager who works at a corporate office. I also informally interviewed three section managers at a food show, which will be described below. In the interviews, I asked these individuals about the work involved in managing a retail food store as well as the sources of information they relied on to help them operate their stores. They stated that they read trade industry publications, general marketing newsletters, specific corporate newsletters, food and beverage magazines, as well as business newspapers such as *The Wall Street Journal*. In addition to analyzing the interviews, I also searched leading trade publications for articles on consumer management including *Progressive Grocer*, *Supermarket News*, the Food Marketing Institute (FMI), which produces research, education, and outreach for food retailers and wholesalers, and the Grocery Manufacturers of America (GMA), which represents the manufacturers of food, beverage, and consumer products.

In this chapter, I will describe the work of managers and how they make decisions such as what products to stock, how to display products, and what to put on sale. I connect these practices with a consumer control discourse transmitted in trade journals and then present how the shoppers I interviewed experienced the retail environment.

MANAGERS AND PRACTICE

The managers I interviewed for this study were all white men, except for one white woman who was the grocery manager at a rural store. All were very willing to talk with me about their jobs, the work for which included ordering and purchasing products, personnel issues like hiring and orientation, construction of advertisements, managing department managers, and customer service. The head managers work long hours, often fifty to sixty hours a week, six days a week. Almost all of them were shoppers themselves. Chris Morris told me he used to do all the shopping until he and his wife had a baby. Now, his wife goes shopping on the one day he has off (Sunday) so he can stay with his daughter. Craig Wallace does about 70 percent of his household's grocery shopping because he believes that he has more knowledge than the average shopper about both price and food in general.

Mike Stephens enjoys shopping. He has been in the business for twenty years and knows how the system works. He jokes that he should go on *The Price is Right* because he knows what the real price is, especially the difference between retail and wholesale, which influences what he buys. He makes his grocery list according to the layout of the store so he can get in and out quickly without forgetting anything. He also knows that the "as advertised" signs are there to get him to gravitate toward an item, and he knows that companies try to get customers to buy in larger quantities because they know you will actually use more. Regarding his job, he says, "It's not the most glamorous thing in the world. It's very simple. It's nothing very hard, just marketing, that's what I do. I sell groceries."

Today, all managers must be in the business of selling groceries if they want to stay in business. In the current retail environment, with profit margins at 1–2 percent and large corporate competitors like Walmart cornering markets, selling groceries means moving a lot of product. Managers must keep up with the plethora of new products that manufacturers roll out—thirty to forty new products each month—as well as confront changes in lifestyles that make cooking at home less convenient. Without knowing what their shopper wants, Stephens argues, managers won't stay in business.

How do managers know what products to stock their shelves with? Frank O'Donnell, a rural store owner, says customer wants drive what he buys; he has been in the business long enough to know what the people in his community want and will buy. For example, his customers (and grocery shoppers in general) want grapes all year round, even when they are out of season, so he makes sure he always has a shipment of grapes, even if they have to come from Mexico. His customers like skinless chicken breasts rather than pork chops, which sell better in the next town.

Chris Morris, manager of the discount store, stated that his customers expect low prices and this shapes how the store is organized. He said:

> We are not about image. We are about cheap groceries, low food prices. We are a case-cut store, which means we cut the tops off the cases and cut out the front and stack them on the shelves. Our customers want and expect low prices.

The assistant manager of the full-service store, Craig Wallace, is much more specific about what drives his product selection. The emphasis of his particular store is customer service. To him, customer service means:

Giving the customer the best price, the best quality of the products that they buy, and the freshness of the products. It is being sure that the folks that greet them at the door are pleasant with them and doing everything to go above and beyond everything that a customer would expect out of a sixteen-year-old sacking groceries or a gentleman in the meat department serving something over the counter. And basically how I understand it is that you are not going to let anyone leave the store unhappy; no matter what you are going to have to do to make them happy, that's what you are going to have to do.

Craig repeatedly stated that product selection is mostly based on customer demand, a statement clearly contradicted by store practices discussed below.

Product placement is one issue that turns out to be less than straightforward and in large measure influenced by food manufacturers and distributors. Manufacturers directly order, stock, and shelf several sections of the grocery store, a practice known as direct store delivery (DSD). Soda, bread, and snack sections are examples of these types of DSD in which a representative of the manufacturing company monitors the shelves, decides where to place the products he delivers, and sets the prices for the products. The store manager has little control over what is on the shelves or how the products are shelved but does benefit by the reduced labor costs of stocking the shelves. Manufacturers also benefit from this arrangement because it allows them to introduce new products without going through the retailer's warehouse.

Manufacturers also get their new products on the shelves through slotting fees. Slotting fee allowances are one-time payments a supplier makes to a retailer as a condition for the initial placement of the new product on the retailer's shelves or space in the retailer's warehouse (Federal Trade Commission 2003). This amount can range anywhere from several hundred dollars for a new product in a single store to several thousand dollars for a chain-wide placement (Food Marketing Institute 2002). Suppliers state that slotting fees are paid on between 80 and 90 percent of all new products (Federal Trade Commission 2003).

Distributors also assign a sales representative to a geographic region for all new product lines and established branded products. These representatives visit stores in their region, ask for their items to be placed on certain shelves and in certain places, and introduce new items to the managers. Chris Morris said he always has sales representatives coming up to him and asking, "Is there any way I can get this on? Can we work this in?" The sales reps are always pitching him new products for a certain demographic. Each item is always represented by a salesman:

> The salesman from Crossmark, a brokerage firm, represents everything from Pillsbury cake mix, Crisco oil, to Hefty plates. They also have independent brokers . . . like one guy works for Shrowd and he has Malto-Meal cereal and I buy ten pallets at a time. He gets a commission off of that somehow. Then you know Proctor and Gamble; they have Tide, Era, Cheer, Bounty, Charmin, and forty percent of the non-food; he comes to see me and that's all he does is Proctor and Gamble. So I buy from him; he sets me up on deals and stuff like that. It's rare that do we not see a salesman walk through the door every day.

Sales representatives also influence where managers place products on the shelves. When asked how he determines product placement and if a section is doing well, Craig Wallace first said it is customer driven but in the next sentence contradicted himself:

> Proctor and Gamble or Kraft or someone that owns a huge portion of an item spread in a section may come out and say "we are running this campaign" or "this is what works best for your demographic let's set it up this way." Look at our room freshener section which would be the Glade candles and plug-ins and things like that. These companies wish it would get bigger. I have eight feet in the store for it and there's probably five or six new items that come out each week that I'm trying to fit into this eight-foot section. If you look at it, it's overwhelmed with fifteen different flavors of apple-blossom plug-in and so at that point you say "do I have to carry Ocean surf and Ocean mist or can I just have one of those"?

Suppliers have also convinced the managers at his store to introduce TVs at this store to air ads for their new products on TVs set up around the store, and Craig is puzzled by the negative comments he's received about the TVs. He asked, "Why wouldn't consumers want more information about products?"

Managers also use strategies to increase sales at the retail level. If an item is not selling well, one manager has found that if he takes it away for a time and then brings it back, customers will be more likely to remember the product and it will sell quickly after that. Signage is also extremely important. Managers report that if they put out a sign that says "new item," especially one sticking out from the grocery shelf, people are more likely to look at it. A sign that shows what looks like a sale but is really a marked-up price is also effective in catching shoppers' eyes. The frozen foods manager at the rural store puts a sign on Banquet dinners that states, "5/$5 on everyday low price," which is actually an 18 percent markup, fooling people into thinking they are getting a sale. Signs that state "10 for $10" also confuse people as customers think they have to buy ten of them.

Where managers place products on the shelves also influences what people buy. When he is "merchandising" his store, Wallace bases where he places products on the shelves by the height of the average American, which is about five feet five inches. People are more likely to buy what they see, and putting the products with the store brand at eye level is most profitable for the store because female retailers can get the store's name onto people's home pantry shelves. Some sections are tailored to specific clientele. Managers "demograph" (Craig Wallace's term) the cereal, candy, and fruit snack aisles for a three-foot person; retailers place the best-selling vitamin and over-the-counter medications on higher shelves so senior citizens don't have to bend down to pick up items.

The layout of the store is not accidental. The physical design of the store is meant to encourage certain patterns of shopping. Foods that provide the largest profits for the store are found at the perimeter of the store, which includes the produce, deli, and meat sections. According to Craig Wallace, the gross margin (the difference between what the store paid for a product and what it charges) is 35 percent on produce while only 15 percent on grocery products (the section in the middle of the store). The grocery section has the least turnover and thus the lowest profit margin. The organization of the store encourages, almost forces, shoppers to enter each of these more profitable sections. The organization of the store also encourages shoppers to make their trips as long as possible by routing them to all the different sections, which means that shoppers are more likely to make unplanned purchases. How much customers buy is directly related to the amount of time they spend in the store (Underhill 1999), so practices that extend shoppers' trips are important to the store's bottom line.

ADVERTISEMENT PRODUCTION

Many shoppers who participated in my study said they used the weekly grocery store advertisements to make their lists for their grocery store trips. Since they identified this text as important to their work, I traced the process by which this text was created for one of the stores in my study. The rural manager was part of the advertising team for his head office, and he stated that the process of making the weekly advertisements begins with a committee of store managers and corporate salespeople who decide three months in advance what products will be on sale. Individual managers can set the prices for products on the front page, but the rest of the ad is standard for all the stores in the cooperative. Occasionally they put a loss-leader on the front page, which is a product that they are selling for less than wholesale cost in order to bring people into the store.

Frank O'Donnell explained that for each item listed in the ad, the supplier pays a marketing fee to the retailer in order to get their product listed and offers a lower wholesale cost to the retailer. The larger ads at the top cost more and get less expensive as you go down the page. Some margin is built into the inside ads so that the store doesn't lose as much as it does on the front page ads.

Frank O'Donnell introduced me to Mike Stephens, the sales manager at the franchise corporate headquarters. Stephens described how an ad is assembled at his level. First, he said, when they create the ad they try to include products from all the departments to entice the customer to shop the entire store; items from produce, bakery, meat, frozen/dairy, grocery, health and beauty, and even floral will appear in every ad. The sales department also attempts to coordinate products so that shoppers will buy more to make a complete meal. For example, if spaghetti sauce is on sale, the logic is that shoppers will also buy spaghetti, or if ground beef is on sale, they will also buy buns.

While he'd like to say that the ad is based on what the customers want, in actuality, "these manufacturers pay us to be in the ad a lot of it is based on what the manufacturer wants which pays for us to print this ad. So it's vendor driven. Our whole marketing division functions by selling these spots in this ad." The manufacturer will not only offer a certain deal to the retailers, for instance, three dollars off a case of Frosted Flakes, but will also pay the marketing department a fee to place its product in the advertisement. The company is making profit on almost every item in the ad, anywhere from 5 percent to 40 percent profit. "If it's in the ad, the manufacturer lowers the cost, we lowered it to the retailer, we lowered the ad retail so everybody wins. We sell groceries, the store sells groceries, and the consumer gets a better price." This quote encapsulates the consumer sovereignty ideology: While it appears this process benefits consumers by providing lower prices, it is clear that manufacturers and retailers are deciding which products get put on the shelves, not consumers. The power of the manufacturers and retailers to choose products was nowhere more evident than at a corporate food show, which I describe below.

THE FOOD SHOW

The food show is a regional food exposition that allows manufacturers to showcase their new food items for possible purchase by the attending managers. These food shows are held roughly four times a year; the particular show that I attended was held at a downtown convention center and featured over 200 vendors, including big manufacturers like Con Agra, Kraft, Nestle, Proctor and Gamble, and Kellogg's, as well as a few regional suppliers. I attended the show with the owner of the rural store, as well as the frozen foods, produce, and meat managers of that store. The store owner estimated that each company paid thousands of dollars per table to be a part of the expo, and some companies like Kraft had ten tables alone. He commented that if companies would eliminate this step they could pass the savings onto the customer. But the frozen food manager stated that it was important for him to see how items would look on a shelf. Each table was decorated with signage and had a representative dressed in corporate attire in front handing out free samples. This show highlighted some of the twenty thousand new products introduced every year and the representatives were very anxious to get the managers to try their new items.

The dairy manager I went with was eager to put new items on his shelf. He said people like to try new things, and the store can charge more because there is no prior reference price for comparison. For example, he told me that regular markup (the difference between wholesale and retail price) on groceries is 15 percent. On meat and produce, the markup is 35 percent due to shrinkage—they factor in perishables arriving spoiled or going bad on the shelf. With new grocery items you can get markups of 20 percent to 25 percent. Another reason the food show is important to the retailers is that they are eligible for an early buying allowance, which means if they buy from the show they will get an additional discount from the manufacturer for prebooking the item at the food show. This is one way manufacturers deal with risk in the market, but the process also squeezes out smaller manufacturers and distributors who cannot offer these discounts.

Managers sampled a wide variety of products, including fruit juice energy drinks, processed cheeses, meats, BBQ pork, Mt. Olive Kosher Dill pickles, and Harley Davidson Beef Jerky. Each time they discussed whether or not the product would sell in their particular store. At every stand they asked, "Will people buy this?" and "Can I sell it?" They passed right by the organic section (the rural clientele is meat and potatoes, they said). As an observer, I was struck by the fact that these people are my purchasing agents and by how little of what is available in the store I as a consumer actually get to see or choose from on my supermarket shelves.

The practices of the managers illustrate that there is a difference between giving customers what they want and organizing the store so that customers will buy certain products, or just more products in general. But we see another level of control in the marketing literature managers say they read. These industry texts advise managers to gather as much information on their customers as they can to build a relationship that will make the customer loyal to the store. While this seems straightforward, this discourse supports management practices that entice shoppers into buying products they might not want, encourage novelty purchases, and disorient shoppers into impulse purchasing.

KNOW YOUR CUSTOMER

To manufacturers and retailers "knowing your shopper" means gathering as much information as possible about the demographics of your customers, what your customers are buying, and what their practices are. Building relationships means finding ways to build customer loyalty. Ultimately, the goal of both messages is the same: regardless of the specific individual needs of the consumer, the retailer wants to get the consumer to buy from them and to buy more product.

Marketers encourage managers to

> know their shoppers through information gleaned from loyalty cards, the cards that customers sign up for to get discounts on purchases in the store as well as on other goods such as gasoline. Retailers use these cards to track consumer purchases and their responses to new promotions. Marketers and retailers also purchase information from companies that compile data based on UPC purchasing (tracked with barcode technology) as well as conduct their own consumer research through surveys, focus groups, and online consumer panels (Karolefski 2007).

Retailers, one article states, are working harder to know their customers' needs and then tailoring promotions accordingly. How do they understand what the shopper needs?

> Retailers analyze loyalty card data and sending color-coded coupon offers to different shoppers depending on their spending behavior. Shopper insights help us understand what a customer is doing in the store. Retailers can then use targeted marketing to "build customer relationships." (Moses 2005a)

Why is knowing your customers and what they "need" so important? According to America's Research Group of Charleston, South Carolina, it costs three to four times as much to attract new customers (using advertising, marketing, and promotions) as it does to retain an old one (Moses 2005a). So creating "relationships" is an important marketing strategy to keep customers in the same store.

In an increasingly competitive retail market, marketers state that knowing and rewarding their most loyal customers is very important. Retailers should identify their best customers and market specifically to those people. Some retailers are doing this through TVs hanging in various aisles through the store, while others do it with sampling or on-site events. Marketers advise managers to market their stores in order to hold onto these loyal customers and actually increase customer spending by targeted promotions (Hamstra and Zwiebach 2005).

Large retailers are also connecting with manufacturers to provide promotions through loyalty cards. For example, customers can download Unilever coupons directly onto the Kroger store card and use these coupons at the checkout line. Kroger's corporate loyalty vice president views "coupons as a way to build customer loyalty by saving them time and money" (Angrisani 2008).

Marketers often conceptualize their customers as "types" of shoppers. One article states that consumers have four "shopping modes" as they cruise the aisles: auto pilot, variety seeking, buzz, or bargain hunting. By understanding these particular shopper modes, the retailer can disrupt consumer behavior through advertising, new offers, prices, and promotions. "Marketers can leverage this brief window of opportunity to trigger change by understanding which hot buttons to push" ("Four Shopping 'Mind-Sets'" 2007). Another marketing manual breaks the consumer up into nine consumer "need states" ranging from "caring for the family," to "stocking up," to "smart budgeting," to "immediate consumption." Using this information, the store manager is expected to determine what "need state" they want to target and then brand the store and brand the image (Coca-Cola Retailing Research Council of North America 2008). Another marketing study divides organic consumers into six categories: health enthusiasts, organic idealists, unengaged shoppers, hog-washers, bargain shoppers, and distrustfuls. The key to reaching this consumer is to target promotions and signage to the different consumer types ("Four Shopping 'Mind-Sets' " 2007).

Marketers tout technology as one of the keys to serving customers. Loyalty cards are very important as they give the retailer an opportunity to monitor food purchases while also tailoring sales. Kroger uses loyalty card data to target promotions based on what the consumer buys. Through a partnership with Dunnhumby, a British loyalty marketing firm, these companies analyze frequent shopper data, segment their best shoppers into different categories, and send them relevant offers and information (Angrisani 2005).

Retailers are using stand-alone counters, known as kiosks, to individualize marketing strategies. One article suggests that retailers should add kiosks throughout the store where the shopper can scan her loyalty card and can see her cumulative savings as well as receive targeted coupons and specials. These offers are for the products the shopper most frequently purchases and related items, and are only available through the Shopping Solutions kiosk. The kiosk is one of a series of promotions, however. Once the shopper gets her coupons, she then is treated to forty-two-inch digital plasma screens in departments like produce and meat/deli, and also audio programming. The marketing manager states that, "We also use the emotion of video and the immediacy of point-of-purchase to bring awareness of products and promotional services." One store that featured this multi-pronged approach to introduce a new product experienced a 131.3 percent increase in sales versus only 86.5 percent at the regular store (Garry 2006).

A chain of stores in San Francisco tried using finger-scan biometric identification instead of digital loyalty cards to provide instant offers at the checkout line to customers as well as make payments. This scanning information was used along with customer e-mail addresses and cell phone numbers to send them targeted sales promotions. Although the technology didn't take off, the goal of the promotions was the same: "By increasing relevancy, we will encourage shoppers to buy more. If you like Pepsi and I like Coke, we can both shop at the same store because discounts are available for both products" (Garry and Mercado 2005).

While technology is touted as a means to increase sales, it also increases the work of the shopper in the store. Not only are self-checkout lines common in most stores, but coming down the pike are hand-held scanners that customers use as they shop. However, retail management states that this added work will benefit shoppers by speeding up the checkout process in addition to allowing shoppers to keep a running tally of their purchases which "reassures shoppers on a fixed budget. Indeed, those shoppers may be empowered to spend more than they would without knowing their total" (Garry and Mercado 2005). Supermarkets may also have a scale that requires shoppers to weigh their own produce and make bar codes by entering price look-up numbers.

The ultimate goal of retailers is not only to reward loyal shoppers but also to shape their behavior, because understanding consumer behavior allows stores to develop strategies to maximize profit. "Through case studies and examples, a deep understanding of consumer shopper behavior will result in the right promotions to maximize lift [sales]" ("Key to Supermarket Growth" 2007). One study titled "Data Mining for Precision Consumer Marketing" examines how retailers' frequent shopper data can be analyzed to pinpoint everything from how loyal a family is to a specific laundry detergent to how often they purchase macaroni and cheese. The study describes how an effective data collection partnership between manufacturers and retailers could potentially increase annual brand sales more than 10 percent while significantly improving the store's bottom line in general and in certain product categories (Grocery Manufacturers of America 2000). This study states in no uncertain terms that consumer data is directly connected to increased profits.

BUILD RELATIONSHIPS

Knowing your shopper is one way to get consumers into the store; understanding what customers want is one way to keep them there. According to one marketer, customers want healthy food at low prices but they are also fickle: "Retailers will be in a stronger position to consistently satisfy the American shopper's constantly changing tastes and buying preferences . . . [retailers] should form a stronger relationship that goes beyond price" (Lempert 2008).

But where do consumers get their changing tastes? Much of this originates in marketing campaigns.

One retail and manufacturing strategy to satisfy needs and build relationships is branding. *Branding* is a standard marketing term that describes the process by which a good or service is associated with a certain brand name. Once the consumer connects the product with a name brand and prefers this brand over others, a relationship has been established. Marketers encourage retailers to make a connection with their customers to keep them coming back by building relationships through branding the store as well as individual products. One marketer stated: "Brands are powerful commodities. The best of them represent more than a product or service—they inhabit those parts of our brain that connect to basic feelings of self-worth, comfort, power, and attractiveness" (MacLeod 2008). This marketer advises retailers to create the right kind of shopping experience for the customer in order to brand their store image.

Walmart, for example, is trying to reposition itself as a good source of healthy products for families. They have introduced a new branding campaign that connects Walmart with an iVillage.Inc website called momtourage.com, a networking group that offers expert advice on mothering issues. Through this marketing campaign Walmart hopes to connect its image with the knowledge of mothers to brand the store as parent-friendly. In-store displays and recorded messages featuring parenting tips will help reinforce the branding message (Gallagher 2008).

Many stores are using the current concern for the environment to create customer loyalty as well as brand stores with a green image. A recent study commissioned by the Grocery Manufacturers of America (2008):

> [G]reen shoppers shop more frequently, buy more per trip, and are to some degree less price sensitive than the average shopper; they should be perceived as gold in the eyes of executives. Since, again based on our survey results, green shoppers tend to become loyal to green products once they've tried them, they should be perceived as platinum in the eyes of consumer products executives.

In order to build relationships with these sought-after consumers, the study advises retailers to send fewer paper-based print materials but rather have an opt-in website to provide direct mail or circulars online that could be easily personalized. Another "green" method of promotion would be a green loyalty program that rewards shoppers for buying green products (Grocery Manufacturers of America 2008).

One marketer advises that stores need to win the loyalty of environmentally conscious shoppers now because soon "ecologically friendly attributes will be a given." The benefits to environmentally conscious branding are significant:

> Retailers hoping to make connections with socially minded consumers can most effectively do so by maintaining transparency while communicating the "tribal" benefit of a particular product. "It's going to be very important that the brand empowers and enables our joining a community of like-minded people that share our values," said Mitch Baranowski, founding partner of BBMG, a New York-based marketing firm. (Hamstra 2008)

Many stores are now eliminating plastic bags and providing cloth bags for purchase. Although one executive suggested that his store's cloth bags were an effort to do the right thing, offering the bags also "helps burnish the company's image in the area of environmental sustainability" (Hamstra 2008).

Branding also allows retailers to make a connection between the customer and the product. Marketers advise retailers to make some kind of emotional connection with shoppers, to

> meet their needs through signage, layout and ambiance. Bundle products by theme—say barbequing—and present them with strong imagery. Entice shoppers to buy store brands by offering samples to taste. (Moses 2005b)

Retailers should use emotional branding as a way to make people feel better about themselves. "People are not going to be buying products just for functional value. They're going to look at products that make a difference in their lives" (Angrisani 2005).

Marketers argue that branding should begin as early as possible to hook consumers. In response to media reports on the rising obesity epidemic, supermarkets are connecting with marketers to brand fruits and vegetables with licensed cartoon characters from Disney and Nickelodeon such as the Incredibles, Dora the Explorer, and SpongeBob SquarePants on the packaging. This campaign is designed to promote healthy eating choices for children by increasing the consumption of fresh fruits and vegetables. But the article ends with a quote from a marketing executive on the benefits of this strategy to the manufacturing companies:

> "If you can get that young child to eat broccoli, for example, you'd hope you're developing a long-term broccoli consumer . . . We need to make sure we're getting

kids hooked on fruits and vegetables as early as possible so we do not only give them a better chance at learning in school and growing up strong and healthy, but also, we're going to build consumers for life . . . somebody who will be eating your products for 60, 70, 80 years," Michelle Poris, director of quantitative research for Just Kid Inc., a Stamford, Conn.-based market research company, said. (Sung 2006)

The consumer control discourse, in essence, standardizes the shopper. Instead of embodied individuals with specific needs, the marketing discourse describes customers as certain demographics and instructs retailers to know their customers and build relationships not with individuals, but a demographic statistic. This marketing process also creates the demand it says it caters to by creating a closed feedback loop—customers don't necessarily buy what they want but what they are told they should want.

NOTES FROM REAL LIFE

The disconnect between the consumer control discourse, retail practice, and shoppers' experience is exposed when you ask consumers not what kind of products they want but how they would like to shop. Unfortunately, I didn't ask all consumers this question but even when I did most could not think of a different way of obtaining food. This lack of imagination of alternatives in food provisioning speaks volumes to the institutional power of our current system.

When I asked shoppers how they liked shopping or what they wished were different, it was not the choice of certain products that they identified, but rather the work process of shopping they discussed. Several shoppers half joked that they would like someone to do the work for them but then added that really they would like some kind of respite from the ongoing work of feeding and provisioning their families. Several shoppers talked about using a meal preparation service through which, for a fee, all the ingredients are bought, chopped, and presented in a store where the shopper becomes the assembler; one or two weeks worth of meals are frozen for later use. Lisa Corbin said that if she were working and had more money she would go to one of those places:

[T]hey make up your food for you and then you can freeze it and have it. I would probably do that. I'm too cheap to do it now. I would have somebody else prepare it so I'm not constantly eating out or my kids aren't always eating out and they are still having good food that is not always just frozen processed food.

Kelly Barnes also expressed an interest in this type of meal making as an alternative to grocery shopping:

It's like 200–300 dollars and you have enough meals for a month, maybe like three to five meals a week for a month; you cook them all and then you freeze them. That would be worth it; that would be awesome to be able to do that.

Other shoppers wanted more time for shopping and cooking. As a professional working mother, Jessica Pierce said:

I don't like to shop. I do enjoy cooking, but right now I don't have time for either. I would definitely spend more time cooking and shopping if I had the time.

April Malloy, another working mother, wanted more balanced meals with vegetables and a little variety. She finds the meals she makes boring and said:

I would have more variety if I had more time to spend in the kitchen or spend at home. More time to julienne my vegetables or to make a side dish with our pasta.

Stacey Ostrander had just switched from part-time to full-time employment when I talked with her about shopping for her household. When she was working part time, she could shop during the day and spent less time on planning; now she plans meals and does shopping trips on weekends and after work. This shopping time (and other household responsibilities) now take the place of spending time with the family. With her voice wavering, she told me that:

We used to play games in the evenings; the errands were done, dinner was earlier and after dinner we would have time to sit around and play cards or play a board game. And that has really fallen by the wayside because we get home later, dinner is later, she has to practice piano for twenty minutes, she has homework, and then its bedtime. And I miss that, I miss the board games, I miss the card games, that's the fun stuff. I feel like we get everything done but that's a fun thing I really miss.

Another group of shoppers identified the organization of shopping as something they would like to change. Colin Moore, for example, finds shopping a chore. For him, shopping at a traditional market where you knew the people you were buying your food from would make it more meaningful. He would also like regional food: "What you ate would be from mother nature, now you can get tomatoes all year round. It's convenient, but is it right?" When I asked if he tries to eat locally, by going to the farmers' market, for example, he stated, "No, we don't have time; everybody has careers and fifty-hour workweeks, even kids who have school and after school programs. So instead we have Applebee's drive thru."

Jill Burnett finds shopping a hassle and dislikes trying to fight the crowds at the end of the work day. She would love to give someone her list and have them shop for her but more realistically she would like a small market in her neighborhood, somewhere she could walk to. Not only would it be smaller and more convenient, it would also be more personable. She offers:

> Maybe you would know the people that work there and have them know you. It would be a better experience. I don't think I'd be listening to the sacking people at Dillon's talk to each other and bicker, which I have heard. I just think it would be a better experience.

CONCLUSION

Taking the standpoint of the shoppers and managers shows consumer sovereignty to be a fiction in two ways. First, in many cases consumers buy not what they necessarily need but what they are marketed. A good example of how marketers create "needs" is illustrated in an article in *Supermarket News*. Three groups, a marketing company,[1] a corporate interest group (the U.S. Potato Board), and the supermarket (not named in the article), worked together to devise a new method to increase potato sales. The goal of this partnership was to get customers to think differently about potatoes. Their solution was to add kiosks next to the produce section with over 100 recipes using potatoes. Sales of potatoes went up 10 percent without having to offer discounts. While these groups may have been responding to customer need, the expressed reason for the campaign was to "drive sales up in a mature category" or, in other words, create a demand that didn't exist before for an established product (Harper 2007).

Although one could argue that selling more potatoes is an innocuous example, it is the disjuncture between the discourse and the lived experience of shopping that is significant. Based on actual retail practices, the customer is certainly not driving the process of grocery shopping. Products on shelves are supported by manufacturing subsidies—manufacturers pay to get their product on shelves, they pay to get in ads, and they employ a large staff of salespeople who promote their products. The physical organization of the grocery store is not designed to make it easier for shoppers to get food on their tables but rather to force shoppers to go through the entire store even to buy a few items. Products and stores are branded to create relationships with customers, and the products on the shelves are not chosen by customers but are selected by management, to say nothing of the lack of involvement of consumers in what actually gets produced.

Grocery stores are designed to keep shoppers in the store as long as possible, because the amount of time shoppers spend in the store is directly correlated with how much money they spend in the store (Underhill 1999). Retail industry discourse, based on the science of marketing, instructs managers to collect as much demographic information on their customers as possible in order to shape their behavior at the grocery store. Managers should brand the store and certain items through marketing campaigns, disrupt the customer through various marketing and store tactics, and encourage impulse buying.

The managers with whom I talked all stated that it is the customers' needs and wants that drive what they do, but their practices show they draw heavily on the industry discourse. First, retailers design the store so that short trips for a couple of items are not possible; in order to get a gallon of milk shoppers are required to walk through the entire store. Managers use signage to disorient the consumer as to the comparative price of items, place items on the shelf for impulse purchasing, and reward loyal customers with special sales.

The practices of managers at the grocery store work in contradiction to both the efficiency and the nutrition discourses. Shoppers must work harder in the planning phase of shopping in order to subvert the retail practices that encourage overbuying and impulse purchasing. The sheer numbers of non-nutritious choices that are given prominent shelf space makes it more difficult for shoppers to resist, especially if they have to take their children with them. But the consumer sovereignty discourse makes the thought and work that goes into the purchase of the shopper and the practice of the manager invisible by equating the needs of the shopper with what they buy. Shoppers' real needs, which they indicate are more time for cooking and shopping and a more pleasurable way to provision, are obscured by the organizing practices of manufacturers, marketers, and managers.

NOTE

1. The marketing company was The Perishables Group, "an independent consulting firm focused on innovation and creating value for clients in the fresh food industry" (www.perishablesgroup.com).

–6–

Competing Discourses and the Work of Food Shopping

In 2008, a few months after I completed the data collection for this research, the worst economic collapse since the Great Depression occurred. Although it has been officially over since 2009, the consequences for Americans are so deep and widespread that people are now in the streets protesting the inequality in American society. Extended unemployment, rising food prices, mortgage failures, and stalled wages have increased the number of working poor and near poor. From 2008 to 2010, the number of Supplemental Nutrition Assistance Program (SNAP) households rose from 12.7 million to 18.6 million (U.S. Department of Agriculture, Food and Nutrition 2011).

While government expenditures on assistance programs have staved off hunger for some (Sherman 2011), what we don't see or hear about is the invisible work behind the scenes to feed individuals in these households. For example, what happens to the $289.61 (the average monthly SNAP benefit per household) once it gets into the household? Somebody uses it to buy groceries, but often the only time we hear about this work is when the shopper is not spending this money wisely; for example, the ubiquitous claims that people using EBT (Electronic Benefit Transfer) cards are buying only ice cream and soda. Institutional ethnography gives us the opportunity to explore the work of provisioning families from the perspective of the people doing it. In our case, we get the opportunity to look at grocery shopping from a perspective often missing in consumption and food studies: the frontline actors themselves, the grocery shoppers.

My entry into this work and the larger food institution was through the experiences of mostly working-class and middle-class mothers in two Midwestern towns, one suburban, one rural. Of course not all perspectives were covered in this study—urbanites have different transportation issues; people of color and immigrants have different food cultures that influence how they provision; the underclass, working, and rural poor often have access issues (Morton et al. 2005); and the division of labor may be negotiated differently in gay households (Carrington 2002). However, the social organization illuminated by my shoppers' experience is one that all shoppers encounter in some form at the supermarket whether or not they have to engage with it. Interviews with the managers of these grocery stores add another layer of analysis in the institutional organization of grocery shopping.

Grocery shopping involves a great deal of mental and manual labor, including planning meals and menus, making lists, doing budgets, arranging schedules, sacking groceries and loading them into the car, and unloading at home. Although there are some signs the division of labor is changing as household demographics change, women are still responsible for the food work in families whether they are in the labor force or not.

Thus, grocery shopping is unpaid labor done for both the household and the market. The strength of institutional ethnography is that we get to see how people's activities and practices are shaped by the decisions and actions of other people in offices far away from the grocery store (Smith 2005: 59). People and organizations in other levels of this institution shape how this work is coordinated and accomplished through textually based discourses. I have identified at least three discourses that organize this work—the efficient housewife, nutrition, and consumer control discourses—which are disseminated in texts such as women's magazines, nutrition pamphlets, industry journals, and television news segments. These discourses are produced by nutritionists, dieticians, consumer science educators, physicians, journalists, and marketers who work in government agencies and for the food industry.

The efficient housewife discourse provides strategies for the household purchaser to economize in order to save money for the household. In order to be efficient, the shopper should make lists, plan meals in advance, comparison shop, eschew convenience over cost savings, clip coupons, and find someone to watch her children so she can negotiate the store alone. The shopper should exhibit a strict discipline so she can make rational decisions for the economic stability of her household and save money through good practices.

The shopper is also in charge of the nutrition of the household and the health of the family becomes her responsibility. Shoppers must contend with a nutrition discourse that demands a certain knowledge of food, a knowledge steeped in the scientific tradition of reducing food to its component nutrients and exhibited as a form of nutritional literacy. Food becomes an equation to be solved: grams of fat plus sugar plus carbohydrates plus calories, all in the correct proportions, equals the right food. Shoppers must know the difference between monounsaturated, saturated, hydrogenated, and trans fat, for example, and look for the right kind of fat in the food they buy. Separating junk from health or bad from good food is the goal of the shopper according to the nutrition discourse.

Managers talk about organizing the grocery store, selecting products, and advertising as though they are merely responding to customer needs and wants. A consumer control discourse, the third discourse shoppers encounter, instructs managers to glean more information about their customers in order to shape their behavior in ways that benefit the store's profit margin. The marketing literature presents ways to entice consumers to buy more through sensory overload, impulse purchasing and getting more information on their customers. Managers enact some of these practices through misleading signage, higher markups on new products, targeted shelf placement, and in-store advertising campaigns.

The consumer control discourse is designed ultimately to control shoppers' purchases in order to benefit the grocery store and manufacturers. A good example of this can be found in a recent article in *Supermarket News* on how to market to different types of food shoppers (Zwiebach 2010). One type of shopper, the list maker or "shoptomizer," corresponds directly to our efficient housewife: an individual who pre-shops by studying ads, coupons, and websites. The writer of this article argues this group of shopper is tricky to engage because they make so many choices before they enter the grocery store but, according to an industry analyst:

> If the market is doing its job, then point-of-purchase programs—tie-in displays, in-store sampling, multiple-buy offers, promotions or other inducements—are likely to prompt even list-makers to beef up their market basket and *buy more than what was on their list*. (emphasis mine)

DISCOURSES IN CONTRADICTION

The above example also reveals one of the paradoxes of these discourses: they are often in contradiction with each other. Retail strategies that encourage impulse purchasing through specific marketing tactics such as providing samples or the 10/$10 promotion are directly contrary to the efficiency discourse. An efficient shopper is not supposed to succumb to these tactics because she has taken the time before entering the store to make her list, comparison shop, and cut her coupons. The goal of the manager, however, is to get her to buy more than she came for.

Efficient shopping isn't necessarily healthy. Convenience foods that women can make in a short amount of time such as Hamburger Helper or casseroles with cream of mushroom soup contain high levels of sodium. Likewise, shopping for healthy food is not necessarily efficient or cost-efficient. The shopper invested in healthy eating may have to make several stops for different foods, shop at farmers' markets for local vegetables, or pay higher prices for organic or whole wheat products. Cooking low-cost healthy meals such as beans and rice is a difficult sell to children, whose tastes often dictate what gets served. Kids are aware that other options exist; why should they eat oatmeal, for example, when they see Reece's Puffs at eye level in the grocery store? The dilemma that Stacey Ostrander faced illustrates this contradiction between efficiency and health: Does she buy the potato chips that she knows are junk when they are on sale so her husband doesn't buy them at full price? Why won't her family choose the fruit she puts on the counter instead of Lay's barbeque potato chips?

The shoppers in my study attempted to navigate the frequent inconsistencies and conflicts in the organization of grocery shopping, of their relationships with the individuals in their families, with food and industry discourses, as well as the material environment of the grocery store. Shoppers who have to stretch their budget often use the efficiency strategies, such as Jane Smith, who buys frozen vegetables instead of fresh vegetables because she has six children to feed. For single mothers, shopping demands efficiency skills in order to feed a household without another adult in the household—which both of these discourses assume. Provisioning a family on $363 a month takes significant planning and usually involves other resources than just the grocery store such as food banks or free school lunches. For single mothers who work, shopping decisions are also about how to use one's time. For Kelly Barnes, she must decide whether to go to several stores to get the best buy (as the efficiency discourse suggests) or to spend time with her three children. Leisure time is often not even a consideration. With nearly 23 percent of U.S. households headed by single mothers (Bianchi 2010), the issue of time and money to spend on provisioning is not insignificant.

Working-class and lower-middle-class shoppers were more likely to pay attention to price while nutrition was mentioned usually in relation to weight loss and some basic knowledge of food groups. Middle-class professional women expressed profound concern about what they are feeding their kids and were more likely to seek out alternative foods like organic or local, which they can often afford. But the anxiety over what they are putting in their kids' bodies is unmistakable in their discussions of food and shopping. Tracey Kennedy's dilemma—should she let Johnny eat ranch dressing so he will also eat his broccoli—speaks to this mother's anxiety over feeding him the right food. However, many of these women are working a full-time job or have a career and cannot devote the time they want to shopping and cooking. April Malloy, who wants to do more cooking, spends much of her time working and commuting; Jessica Pierce would go to the farmers' market but can't reconcile her working hours with the hours the market is open. The intensive mothering discourse and food critics might argue these mothers just don't have their priorities in order.

SOCIAL ORGANIZATION OF THE ECONOMY

In a neoliberal economy, it is not the polity or the community but the family and ultimately mothers who are responsible for children's well-being. The discourses I've uncovered point to a social organization that depends on women's labor but often makes this work invisible *and* more challenging. While families are the direct beneficiaries of women's food work in the household, the state and the retail store benefit as well. For example, women who utilize the efficiency strategies can spend more money on other consumer goods, which is important in that two-thirds of our nation's gross domestic product is derived from the purchase of consumer goods (Heilbroner and Thurow 1994). Those women who receive taxpayer money through food stamps and can use it wisely become model citizens. As state responsibility for low-income families shifted in the 1990s from entitlement to employment under the Personal Responsibility and Work Opportunity Act (Orloff 2002), shopping efficiently became even more important for the household. The retreat of the state in supplementing household incomes has meant greater reliance on the wage, and as that has contracted in the last couple of years, provisioners must now use many efficiency strategies just to put food on the table, let alone save money for other consumer goods.

The nutrition discourse, which makes individuals responsible for choosing the right nutrients in their food, is only necessary in an industrial agricultural regime that produces non-nutritious food. The goal of our agricultural system is to produce quantity over quality and to encourage only certain agricultural products through the use of synthetic fertilizers, pesticides, and monocultures (Lang 2012). Corn yields, for example, have increased from 54.7 bushels per acre in 1960 to 161.9 bushels per acre in 2009 (Iowa State Extension 2010). Federal subsidies support five commodity crops and almost no organic food or fruits or vegetables (Nestle 2002), and the Farm Bill promotes large factory farms over small, local farms or alternative agricultural methods. High fructose corn syrup, which the nutrition discourse tells shoppers to avoid, is a logical outcome of an industrial system that is chemical-based and produces mega-tons of a single product. Pollan and other food critics zero in on this disjuncture between what we subsidize and what we produce, but then leave the responsibility on the consumer to make wise choices once these products are already in the food system.

GENDERED ECONOMY

Looking at the social organization of food shopping from the standpoint of the shopper suggests that grocery shopping is not organized to benefit shoppers but instead devolves responsibility to shoppers for their individual choices. Michael Maniates (2009) argues that a consumer sovereignty ideology breeds this "individualization" in which responsibility for all consumption-related problems is attributed to freestanding individuals. In this approach the social organization and social forces that influence what and how people act are ignored. Individual choice-makers are not only deprived of important knowledge they may need, they are also cut off from decisions made in other parts of the institution. Thus, solutions to social problems become the responsibility of the individual. The obesity debate and solutions are a good example of individualization (Szasz 2007). Industrial food (processed, low nutrition) has been identified as one of the obesity culprits, but instead of removing these foods from the production cycle which results in people consuming them, the individual is responsible for avoiding them once they are already on the shelf.

In our case, an ideology of intensive mothering in the standard North American family not only individualizes solutions but intensifies the responsibility for producing healthy children for a certain category of people: mothers. This dilemma for provisioners points to problems with the neoliberal conceptualization of the economy as a market activity undertaken by satisfaction-seeking individuals, a model that ignores important structural characteristics that affect one's ability to provision for households such as gender, race, class, sexuality, and nationality (Acker 2006). Feminists argue that one way to remedy this inaccurate conceptualization is to redefine the goal of economic activity. Julie Nelson defines economic activity as "the provisioning of human life, that is, the commodities and processes necessary to human survival" (1993: 32). This definition includes unpaid care work, volunteer work, and subsistence work in addition to paid labor and opens up wider possibilities for theorizing economic processes. By not including unpaid labor including acts such as grocery shopping in our theories of economy, corporations and the state are absolved of their responsibility for provisioning in a neoliberal economy under the auspices of consumer sovereignty (Acker 2006).

The larger food institution, which includes government agencies, media, food manufacturers and retailers, and farmers, depends on the work of shoppers. However, this institution does not include shoppers in making important decisions about what kind of food is produced and how it is grown, how food gets distributed and put on the shelves, or even fundamental questions like whether the supermarket strategy is the best way to produce healthy individuals. If we start from the standpoint of the grocery shopper and work from her needs, we can then begin to imagine an alternate social organization that will be more effective at provisioning our households.

Critics of the agrofood system have already suggested avenues to rethink our relationship to food provisioning. Fresh, quality food should be a human right divorced from one's relationship to the market (Allen 1999). Consumption must be reconceptualized from a passive act of final purchasing to an active partnership between public governance, citizen consumers, and producers (McMahon 2011). But while these solutions may increase access or quality, they do not necessarily relieve women, especially mothers, of the responsibility of procuring and preparing food. The division of labor in the household for feeding families must be addressed. Men must begin to shoulder more responsibility for food work at all levels. The structure of paid work must be flexible enough or even be scheduled around our responsibilities for provisioning. A more controversial solution is to take provisioning out of the household altogether, and make it a public responsibility.

Tracey Deutsch suggests specific examples of how to reimagine the social organization of food provisioning in ways that would make it easier for people to feed their families as well as open space for more public provisioning. What if, she asks,

> food was purchased in small increments from neighborhood peddlers who brought it to your door? What if school lunch programs were extended to work sites and neighborhood centers so that adults could eat it too? What if working hours were uniformly cut so that people could attend to all sorts of nonwage-earning commitments? What if everyone earned enough money that they didn't have to worry about affording food? What if food were not a commodity at all? (Deutsch 2011)

These are radical solutions in an era when the market dominates our possibilities for provisioning. If healthy people and bodies is our goal, however, we will need to explore these options.

Appendix

Table A.1 Interview Demographics

Pseudonyms	Age	Education (Years)	Household Income	Number of Children in Home	Marital Status	Community Type	Employment
Jackie Engle	33	12+	60,000	3	M	Rural	Full-time
Jane Smith	32	12+	45,000	6	M	Rural	Part-time
Karen Calhoun	48	12	20,000	3	M	Rural	Stay at Home
Peggy Fiske	28	12	13,000	2	S	Rural	Stay at Home
Kelly Barnes	39	18	40,000	3	S	Rural	Full-time
Maggie Waggoner	42	18	90,000	2	M	Rural	Full-time
April Malloy	41	18	90,000	2	M	Rural	Full-time
Jessica Pierce	39	18	95,000	3	M	Suburban	Full-time
Meg Moore	31	18	65,000	1	M	Suburban	Part-time
Kay Worthington	45	18	100,000	3	M	Suburban	Part-time
Karen Jones	33	18	70,000	2	M	Suburban	Stay at Home
Colin Moore (male)	30	18	65,000	1	M	Suburban	Full-time
Jill Burnett	35	16	35,000	0	S	Suburban	Full-time
Lisa Corbin	32	16	40,000	4	M	Suburban	Part-time
Melissa Long	50	12	85,000	0	M	Rural	Full-time
Lorraine Kinney	65	16	65,000	0	M	Suburban	Retired
Jeanne McCoy	82	16	40,000	0	Widow	Rural	Retired
Stacey Ostrander	50	16	90,000	1	M	Suburban	Full-time
Susie Zimmerman	32	12	45,000	2	M	Rural	Full-time
Stacy Taylor	39	16	100,000	2	M	Suburban	Full-time
Frank O'Donnell							Manager/ owner
Mike Stephens							Sales manager
Craig Wallace							Retail manager
Chris Morris							Retail manager

Bibliography

Acker, Joan. 2006. *Class Questions, Feminist Answers*. Lanham, MD: Rowman and Littlefield Publishers, Inc.

Alfano, Sean. 2005. "No Ordinary Trip to the Market." *CBS Sunday Morning*, November. Accessed August 25, 2008. http://www.cbsnews.com/stories/2005/11/20/sunday/main1060317.shtml?tag=contentMain;contentBody.

Allen, Patricia. 1999. "Reweaving the Food Security Safety Net: Mediating Entitlement and Entrepreneurship." *Agriculture and Human Values* 16: 117–29.

Allen, Patricia, and C. Sachs. 2007. "Women and Food Chains: The Gendered Politics of Food." *International Journal of Sociology of Food and Agriculture* 15(1): 1–23.

American Dietetic Association. 2003. "Shopping Solutions for Healthful Eating (Nutrition Fact Sheet)." *Journal of the American Dietetic Association* 103(3): 410.

American Dietetic Association. 2005. "Nutrition Fact Sheet: Eating Better Together." Accessed June 24, 2012. http://www.wellnessproposals.com/nutrition/nutrition_fact_sheets/eating_better_together_family_guide_for_a_healthier_lifestyle.pdf.

American Dietetic Association. 2006a. "What's A Mom to Do: Healthy Eating Tips for Families." Accessed June 24, 2012. http://www.harrison.k12.ms.us/LinkClick.aspx?fileticket=6fsRX4qglZs%3D&tabid=62&mid=1190.

American Dietetic Association. 2006b. "Nutrition Fact Sheet: Get Smart–Get the Facts on Food Labels." Accessed June 24, 2012. http://www.eatright.org/Public/content.aspx?id=206.

American Dietetic Association. 2006c. "Nutrition Fact Sheet: Dietary Facts: Clarifying an Age-Old Issue." Accessed June 24, 2012. http://www.wellnessproposals.com/nutrition/nutrition_fact_sheets/dietary_fats_clarifying_an_age_old_issue.pdf.

Angrisani, Carol. 2005. "What's in Store for Brands? Driving Brand Equity at the Point of Purchase Will Take on Greater Importance over the Next Few Years." *Supermarket News*, November 28. Accessed August 23, 2008. http://supermarketnews.com/archive/whats-store-brands.

Angrisani, Carol. 2008. "Savings Simplified." *Supermarket News*, June 23. Accessed August 26, 2008. http://supermarketnews.com/center-store/savings-simplified.

Bauer, Joy. 2012. "The Myths and Facts about Brown Sugar." Accessed January 2012. http://www.joybauer.com/newsletter/myth-and-fact-about-sugar.aspx?xid=nl_JoyBauersDailyPlumNewsletter_20110617.

Bianchi, Susan M. 2009. " 'What Gives' When Mothers Are Employed? Parental Time Allocation in Dual- and Single-earner Two Parent Families." In *Handbook of*

Families and Work, ed. D. Russell Crane and E. Jeffrey Hill, 123–45. Lanham, MD: University Press of America.

Bianchi, Susan M. 2010. "Family Change and Time Allocation in American Families." Paper presented at Focus on Workplace Flexibility conference, November, Washington DC.

Bianchi, Susan M., Melissa A. Milkie, Liana C. Sayer, and John P. Robinson. 2000. "Is Anyone Doing Housework? Trends in the Gender Division of Household Labor." *Social Forces* 79: 191–228.

Bittman, Mark. 2011. "Food Manifesto for the Future." *New York Times*, February 2.

Blanchard, Troy C., and Thomas A. Lyson. 2002. "Retail Concentration, 'Food Deserts,' and Food-Disadvantaged Communities." U.S. Department of Agriculture, Food Assistance and Nutrition Research Report No. 43.

Boland, M.A., and S.K. Schumacher. 2005. "The Sustainability of Return on Assets Among Sectors in the Food Economy." *Agricultural Finance Review* 65(1).

Bowlby, Rachel. 1997. "Supermarket Futures." In *The Shopping Experience*, ed. Pasi Falk and Colin Campbell, 92–110. London: Sage.

Brown, Damon. 2003. "Many Nutritional Opportunities Available through Supermarket Research." *Journal of the American Dietetic Association* 103(4): 453.

Carrington, Christopher. 2002. *No Place Like Home: Relationships and Family Life Among Lesbians and Gay Men*. Chicago: University of Chicago Press.

Casey, Emma, and Lydia Martins, eds. 2007. *Gender and Consumption: Domestic Cultures and the Commercialisation of Everyday Life*. Aldershot: Ashgate.

Centers for Disease Control and Prevention. 2011. "Basics about Childhood Obesity." Accessed April 2012. http://www.cdc.gov/obesity/childhood/basics.html.

Charles, Nicki, and Marion Kerr. 1988. *Women, Food and Families*. Manchester, UK: Manchester University Press.

Churchill, Gilbert A., Jr., and J. Paul Peter. 1995. *Marketing: Creating Value for Customers*. Burr Ridge, IL: Richard D. Irwin.

Coca-Cola Retailing Research Council of North America. 2008. "The World According to Shoppers." January 4. Accessed August 25, 2008. http://www.fmi.org/facts_figs/conference_pdfs/World_According_Shoppers.pdf#search=%22grocery%20shopping%22.

Cohen, Lizabeth. 2004. *A Consumers' Republic: The Politics of Mass Consumption in Postwar America*. New York: Vintage Books.

Coltrane, Scott. 1997. *Gender and Families*. Thousand Oaks, CA: Alta Mira Press.

Cooperative State Research, Education and Extension Service (USDA). 2006. "Expanded Food and Nutrition Education Program Success Stories—Food Resource Management." Accessed October 2006. http://www.csrees.usda.gov/nea/good/efnep/success-foodresource.html.

Cowan, Ruth Schwartz. 1983. *More Work for Mother*. New York: Basic Books.

Crotty, Patricia A. 1995. *Good Nutrition: Fact and Fashion in Dietary Advice*. St. Leonards, NSW, Australia: Allen & Unwin Pty Ltd.

Dawson, Michael. 2003. *The Consumer Trap: Big Business Marketing in American Life*. Urbana: University of Illinois Press.

Deutsch, Tracey. 2002. "Untangling Alliances: Social Tensions Surrounding Independent Grocery Stores and the Rise of Mass Retailing." In *Food Nations: Selling Taste in Consumer Societies*, ed. Warren Belasco and Philip Scranton, 156–74. New York: Routledge.

Deutsch, Tracey. 2010. *Building a Housewife's Paradise: Gender, Politics and American Grocery Stores in the Twentieth Century*. Chapel Hill: University of North Carolina Press.

Deutsch, Tracey. 2011. "Memories of Mothers in the Kitchen: Local Foods, History, and Women's Work." *Radical History Review* 110: 167–77.

DeVault, Marjorie. 1991. *Feeding the Family*. Chicago: University of Chicago Press.

DeVault, Marjorie, and Lisa McCoy. 2007. "Interviewing for Institutional Ethnography." In *Institutional Ethnography as Practice*, ed. Dorothy Smith, 17–33. New York: Rowman & Littlefield Publishers.

Devine, Carol M., Margaret Connors, Jeffery Sobal, and Carole Bisogni. 2003. "Sandwiching It In: Spillover of Work onto Food Choices and Family Roles in Low- and moderate-income Urban Households." *Social Science and Medicine* 56(3): 617–30.

Dixon, Jane. 1999. *The Changing Chicken: Chooks, Cooks, and Culinary Culture*. Sydney: UNSW Press.

Dixon, Jane. 2007. "Supermarkets as New Food Authorities." In *Supermarkets and Agri-food Supply Chains: Transformation in the Production and Consumption of Foods*, ed. David Burch and Geoffry Lawrence, 20–50. Cheltenham, UK: Edward Elgar.

Dixon, Jane, and Cathy Banwell. 2004. "Re-embedding Trust: Unraveling the Construction of Modern Diets." *Critical Public Health* 14(2): 117–31.

DuPuis, E., and David Goodman. 2005. "Should We Go 'Home' to Eat? Toward a Reflexive Politics of Localism." *Journal of Rural Studies* 21(3): 359–71.

Ehrenreich, Barbara, and Arlie Hochschild, eds. 2002. *Global Woman: Nannies, Maids, and Sex Workers in the New Economy*. London: Granta Books.

England, Paula, and Nancy Folbre. 2005. "Gender and Economy." In *The Handbook of Economic Sociology*, ed. Neil J. Smelser and Richard Swedberg, 627–49. Princeton, NJ: Princeton University Press.

Federal Trade Commission. 2003. "The Use of Slotting Allowances in the Retail Grocery Industry: A Report from the Staff of the Federal Trade Commission." Accessed November 15, 2007. http://www.ftc.gov/opa/2003/11/slottingallowance.shtm.

Feldman, Shira, et al. 2007. "Associations between Watching TV during Family Meals and Dietary Intake Among Adolescents." *Journal of Nutrition Education and Behavior* 39(5): 257–63.

Ferber, Marianne, and Julie A. Nelson, eds. 1993. *Beyond Economic Man: Feminist Theory and Economics*. Chicago: Chicago University Press.

Flamming, Janet. 2009. *The Taste for Civilization: Food, Politics, and Civil Society*. Urbana: University of Illinois Press.

Folbre, Nancy. 2002. *The Invisible Heart: Economics and Family Values*. New York: The New Press.

Food Marketing Institute. 2002. "Slotting Allowances in the Supermarket Industry." Accessed October 2008. http://www.fmi.org/media/bg/slottingfees2002.pdf.

Food Marketing Institute. 2005. "U.S Grocery Shoppers Trends." Accessed August 25, 2009.http://www.fmi.org/news_releases/index.cfm?fuseaction=mediatext&id=739.

Food Marketing Institute. 2007. "Food Retailing in the 21st Century—Riding a Consumer Revolution." Accessed August 25, 2009. http://www.fmi.org/docs/media/bg/FoodRetailing.pdf.

Food Marketing Institute. 2009. "Supermarket Facts." Accessed August 25, 2009. http://www.fmi.org/facts_figs/?fuseaction=superfact.

Food Marketing Institute. 2010. "FMI Grocery Shopper Trends 2010: Consumers Are Savvy and Informed Bargain Hunters When it Comes to Grocery Shopping." Accessed May 2010. http://www.fmi.org/news_releases/index.cfm?fuseaction=mediatext&id=1172.

Food Marketing Institute. 2011. "U.S. Grocery Shopper Trends, 2011." Accessed October 15, 2011. http://www.fmi.org/news_releases/index.cfm?fuseaction=mediatext&id=1236.

Food Trust. 2003. "Food Geography: How Food Access Affects Diet and Health: The Need for more Supermarkets in Philadelphia." Accessed May 15, 2007. http://www.thefoodtrust.org/php/programs/super.market.campaign.php#3.

"Four Shopping 'Mind-Sets' Determine How Consumers Shop Supermarkets: Study." 2007. *Progressive Grocer*, May. Accessed October 15, 2008. http://find.galegroup.com.www2.lib.ku.edu:2048/gtx/infomark.do?&contentSet=IAC-Documents&type=retrieve&tabID=T003&prodId=ITOF&docId=A167666199&source=gale&srcprod=ITOF&userGroupName=ksstate_ukans&version=1.0.

Franklin, A. 2001. "The Impact of Wal-Mart Supercenters on Supermarket Concentration in U.S. Metropolitan Areas." *Agribusiness* 17(1): 104–14.

Friedman, Andrew. 2007. "Shopping on a Shoestring." Accessed September 25, 2007. http://www.ivillage.com/shopping-shoestring/3-a-57778.

Galbraith, John Kenneth. 2004. *The Economics of Innocent Fraud: Truth for Our Time*. Boston: Houghton Mifflin Company.

Gallagher, Julie. 2008. "Retailers Trust That Mothers Know Best." *Supermarket News,* July 28. Accessed November 17, 2008. http://supermarketnews.com/center-store/retailers-trust-mothers-know-best.

Garry, Michael. 2006. "Making Connections: Supervalu's Avenu Program Brings Together a Variety of In-Store Electronic Devices, Including Kiosks, Screens and Coupon Printers to Connect with Individual Shoppers." *Supermarket News,* October 23. Accessed August 2007. http://supermarketnews.com/archive/making-connections.

Garry, Michael, and Darla Mercado. 2005. "A Mixed Bag: There's a Lot of New In-store Technology to be Excited About, But Retailers Need to be Wary about Myriad Threats to Their Infrastructure." *Supermarket News,* December 12. Accessed August 2007. http://supermarketnews.com/archive/mixed-bag.

Gates, Kelly. 2008. "Taking Action." *Supermarket News,* August 23. Accessed August 28, 2009. http://find.galegroup.com.www2.lib.ku.edu:2048/gtx/infomark.do?&contentSet=IAC-Documents&type=retrieve&tabID=T003&prodId=ITOF&docId=A183537531&source=gale&srcprod=ITOF&userGroupName=ksstate_ukans&version=1.0.

Gibbons, Vera. 2007. "Sticker Shock at the Grocery Store? Tips on Saving." *Today Show,* August 23. Accessed September 25, 2008. http://today.msnbc.msn.com/id/20412584/print/1/displaymode/1098.

Gillman M. W., S. L. Rifas-Shiman, A. L. Frazier, H. R. Rockett, C. A. Camargo Jr., A. E. Field, C. S. Berkey, and G. A. Colditz. 2000. "Family Dinner and Diet Quality Among Older Children and Adolescents." *Archives of Family Medicine* 9: 235–40.

Glasner, Barry. 2007. *The Gospel of Food.* New York: HarperCollins.

Glazer, Nona Y. 1993. *Women's Paid and Unpaid Labor: The Work Transfer in Health-care and Retailing.* Philadelphia: Temple University Press.

Goldstein, Carolyn M. 2006. "Educating Consumers, Representing Consumers: Reforming the Marketplace through Scientific Expertise at the Bureau of Home Economics, United States Department of Agriculture." In *The Expert Consumer: Associations and Professionals in Consumer Society,* ed. Alain Chatroit, Marie-Emmanuelle Chessel, and Matthew Hilton, 73–88. London: Ashgate.

Goodman, David. 2003. "The Quality 'Turn' and Alternative Food Practices: Reflections and Agenda." *Journal of Rural Studies* 19(1): 1–7.

Goodman, David, and Michael Redclift. 1991. *Refashioning Nature: Food, Ecology and Culture.* New York: Routledge.

Greer, William. 1986. *America the Bountiful: How the Supermarket Came to Main Street.* Washington, DC: Food Marketing Institute.

Griffith, Allison, and Dorothy Smith. 2005. *Mothering for Schooling.* New York: RoutledgeFalmer.

Grocery Manufacturers of America. 2000. "Data Mining for Precision Consumer Marketing." Accessed August 15, 2007. http://www.gmabrands.com/news/docs/NewsRelease.cfm?docid=556.

Grocery Manufacturers of America. 2008. "Delivering the Promise of Shopper Marketing: Mastering Execution for Competitive Advantage." Accessed November 15, 2009. http://www.gmaonline.org/downloads/research-and-reports/GMA-Deloitte_ShopperMktReport_FINAL.pdf.

Guthman, Julie. 2004. *Agrarian Dreams: The Paradox of Organic Farming in California*. Berkeley: University of California Press.

Guthman, Julie. 2007. "Commentary on Teaching Food: Why I Am Fed Up with Michael Pollan et al." *Agriculture and Human Values* 24: 261–64.

Hammock, Delia. 2007. "The ABCs of Vitamin D." *Good Housekeeping*, May: 46.

Hamstra, Mark. 2008. "Supermarkets Make the Most of Reusable Bags." *Supermarket News* 56(28): 18.

Hamstra, Mark, and Elliot Zwiebach. 2005. "Survival Strategies: Supermarket Companies May Need to Rethink their Operations in 2006 to Face a Changing Marketplace." *Supermarket News*, December 12. Accessed August 25, 2007. http://supermarketnews.com/archive/survival-strategies.

Harper, Roseanne. 2007. "Study: Recipe Kiosks Drive Potato Sales." *Supermarket News*, July 30. Accessed July 25, 2008. http://supermarketnews.com/marketing/study-recipe-kiosks-drive-potato-sales.

Haspel, Tamar. 2006. "Insider Tips for Finding and Buying the Healthiest Groceries." *Prevention Magazine*, January 1. Accessed December 5, 2006. http://www.prevention.com/food/smart-shopping/smart-grocery-shopping-guide?page=2.

Hayden, Delores. 2002. *Redesigning the American Dream: Gender, Housing and Family Life*. New York: W.W. Norton & Company.

Hays, Sharon. 1996. *The Cultural Contradictions of Motherhood*. Cambridge, MA: Yale University Press.

Heilbroner, Robert, and Lester Thurow. 1994. *Economics Explained*. New York: Touchstone Books.

Hennen, Leah. 2006. "Smart Grocery Shopping Tips." *Health*, September. Accessed December 5, 2006. http://www.health.com/health/printarticle/0,23478,1540959,00.html.

Henry, Erin, and Mary Meck Higgins. 2006. "Dining on a Dime: Eating Better for Less." August/September newsletter of K-State Research and Extension Family Nutrition Program. Accessed August 2008. http://www.ksre.ksu.edu/HumanNutrition/p.aspx?tabid=91.

Hochshild, Arlie. 1989. *The Second Shift*. New York: Viking.

Hook, Jennifer L. 2006. "Care in Context: Men's Unpaid Work in 20 Countries, 1965–2003." *American Sociological Review* 71: 639–60.

"How to Make the Most of Grocery Shopping." 2008. Associated Press, January 2. Accessed February 12, 2008. http://today.msnbc.msn.com/id/22472157/ns/today-food/t/how-make-most-grocery-shopping/.

Humphery, Kim. 1998. *Shelf Life: Supermarkets and the Changing Cultures of Consumption*. Cambridge: Cambridge University Press.

Humphreys, Sarah. 2004. "Organize Your Grocery Shopping Trips." *Real Simple*.

Iowa State Extension. 2010. "Corn and Soybeans: Harvested Acreage and Yield Per Acre." Accessed August 5, 2011. http://www2.econ.iastate.edu/outreach/agriculture/periodicals/chartbook/Chartbook2/Tables/Table10.pdf.

Jacobs, Jerry A., and Kathleen Gerson. 2001. "Overworked Individuals or Overworked Families? Explaining Trends in Work, Leisure and Family Time." *Work and Occupations* 28(1): 40–63.

Jaffee, JoAnn, and Michael Gertler. 2006. "Victual Vicissitudes: Consumer Deskilling and the (Gendered) Transformation of Food Systems." *Agricultural and Human Values* 23: 143–62.

Janoff, Barry. 2000. "Targeting Consumer Behavior." *Progressive Grocer*, April: 36–43.

Jibrin, Janis. 2007. "Avoiding Grocery Store Temptation." Accessed April 19, 2007. http://www.weightwatchers.com/util/art/index_art.aspx?tabnum=1&art_id=48891&sc=3017#Story.

Johnston, Josée, and Michelle Szabo. 2011. "Reflexivity and the Whole Food Market Shopper: Shopping for Change, or Cruising for Pleasure?" *Agriculture and Human Values* 28: 303–19.

Kantor, Jodi. 2007. "As Obesity Fight Hits the Cafeteria, Many Fear a Note From School." *New York Times*, January 8.

Karolefski, John. 2007. "Giant Food Stores Leverages Consumer Insights." *Supermarket News*, July 30. Accessed August 26, 2008. http://supermarket news.com/retail-amp-financial/giant-food-stores-leverages-consumer-insights.

Kaufman, Phil. 2002. "Food Retailing." Economic Research Service/USDA. Accessed August 28, 2008. http://www.ers.usda.gov/publications/aer811/aer811e.pdf.

"Key to Supermarket Growth is Appealing to Best Customers: Study." 2007. *Progressive Grocer*, July 27. Accessed November 15, 2008. http://www.progressivegrocer.com/top-stories/headlines/industry-intelligence/id23049/key-to-supermarket-growth-is-appealing-to-best-customers-study/.

Konefal, Jason, Carmen Bain, Michael Mascarenhas, and Lawrence Busch. 2007. "Supermarkets and Supply Chains in North America." In *Supermarkets and Agri-food Supply Chains: Transformation in the Production and Consumption of Foods*, ed. David Burch and Geoffry Lawrence, 268–89. Cheltenham, UK: Edward Elgar.

Kramer, Pamela. 2008. "50 Ways to Save." *Woman's Day*, July. Accessed December 5, 2009. http://www.womansday.com/life/saving-money/50-ways-to-save-1708?click=main_sr#slide-1.

Krantz-Kent, Rachel. 2009. "Measuring Time Spent in Unpaid Household Work: Results from the American Time Use Survey." *Monthly Labor Review*, July: 46–59.

Lang, Tim. 2012. "Food Industrialization and Food Power: Implications for Food Governance." In *Taking Food Public: Redefining Foodways in a Changing World*, ed. Psyche Williams-Forson and Carole Counihan, 11–22. New York: Routledge.

Lawrence, Geoffry, and David Burch. 2007. "Understanding Supermarkets and Agri-food Supply Chains." In *Supermarkets and Agri-food Supply Chains: Transformation in the Production and Consumption of Foods*, ed. David Burch and Geoffry Lawrence, 1–28. Cheltenham, UK: Edward Elgar.

Lempert, Phil. 2007a. "The 5-Minute Shopping List." Accessed February 26. http://supermarketguru.com/page.cfm/355.

Lempert, Phil. 2007b. "Home Remedies: Are Grocers Doing All They Can to Help Shoppers Eat Better at the Kitchen Table?" *Progressive Grocer*, August 1.

Lempert, Phil. 2008. "How and Why America Shops!" *Marketing Solutions* (Second Quarter). Accessed August 2009. http://marketingsolutions.valassis.com/story.aspx?url=2008/2008q2_lempert.aspx.

Levenstein, Harvey. 1988. *Revolution at the Table: The Transformation of the American Diet*. New York: Oxford University Press.

Levenstein, Harvey. 2003. *Paradox of Plenty: A Social History of Eating in Modern America*. Berkeley: University of California Press.

Liu, Yvonne Yen, and Dominique Apollon. 2011. "The Color of Food." Applied Research Center, February. Accessed June 24, 2012. http://www.arc.org/content/view/2229/136/.

Lockie, Stewart. 2002. "The Invisible Mouth: Mobilizing 'the Consumer' in Food Production-consumption Networks." *Sociologia Ruralis* 42(4): 278–94.

MacLeod, Leo. 2008. "Just the Right Size: Big Brand Power has Helped these 'Little' Operators." *Progressive Grocer*, February 1. Accessed August 26, 2008. http://global.factiva.com.www2.lib.ku.edu:2048/ha/default.aspx.

Mancino, Lisa, and Constance Newman. 2007. "Who Has Time To Cook? How Family Resources Influence Food Preparation." United States Department of Agriculture, Economic Research Report Number 40. Accessed March 2011. http://www.ers.usda.gov/publications/err40/err40.pdf.

Maniates, Michael. 2009. "Individualization: Plant a Tree, Buy a Bike, Save the World?" In *Environmental Sociology: From Analysis to Action*, ed. Leslie King and Deborah McCarthy, 371–95. Lanham, MD: Rowan and Littlefield Publishers.

Marsden, T. K., and N. Wrigley. 2001. "Regulation, Retailing and Consumption." In *Retailing: Critical Concepts*, ed. Anne M. Findlay and Leigh Sparks, 228–46. London: Routledge.

Mattera, Philip. 2004. "USDA INC: How Agribusiness has Hijacked Regulatory Policy at the U.S. Department of Agriculture." Agribusiness Accountability Initiative and Corporate Research Project, Good Jobs First. Accessed November 2008. http://www.nffc.net/Issues/Corporate%20Control/USDA%20INC.pdf.

Mayo, James. 1993. *The American Grocery Store*. Westport, CT: Greenwood Press.

McMahon, Martha. 2011. "Standard Fare or Fairer Standards: Feminist Reflections on Agri-food Governance." *Agriculture and Human Values* 28: 401–12.

McMichael, Phillip, and Harriett Friedmann. 2007. "Situating the Retail Revolution." In *Supermarkets and Agri-food Supply Chains: Transformation in the Production and Consumption of Foods*, ed. David Burch and Geoffry Lawrence, 294–323. Cheltenham, UK: Edward Elgar.

McTaggart, Jenny. 2005. "Diversified Investment." *Progressive Grocer*, June 1. Accessed August 26, 2008. http://vnweb.hwwilsonweb.com.www2.lib.ku.edu:2048/hww/results/external_link_maincontentframe.jhtml?_DARGS=/hww/results/results_common.jhtml.44

"Meal Planning and Shopping." 2006. USDA Food and Nutrition Services. http://www3.ag.purdue.edu/counties/elkhart/Documents/Participant%20Packet%20Meal%20Plan%202010.pdf.

Mendoza, Martha. 2007. "Review: Nutrition Education Short on Results." *Salina Journal*, July 5.

Miller, Daniel. 1995. "Consumption as the Vanguard of History: A Polemic by the Way of an Introduction." In *Acknowledging Consumption*, ed. Daniel Miller, 1–57. London: Routledge.

Miller, Daniel. 1998. *A Theory of Shopping*. Ithaca, NY: Cornell University Press.

Miranda, V. 2011. "Cooking, Caring and Volunteering: Unpaid Work around the World." OECD Social, Employment and Migration Working Papers, No. 116. OECD Publishing. Accessed May 2011. http://dx.doi.org/10.1787/5kghrjm8s142-en.

Morton, Lois Wright, Ella Bitto, Mary Jane Oakland, and Mary Sand. 2005. "Solving the Problems of Iowa Food Deserts: Food Insecurity and Civic Structure." *Rural Sociology* 70(1): 94–112.

Moses, Lucia. 2005a. "Making their Mark: Technology and Loyalty Marketing are Helping Retailers Forge a Connection with Shoppers in the Center of the Store." *Supermarket News*, December 12. Accessed August 12, 2007. http://supermarketnews.com/archive/making-their-mark.

Moses, Lucia. 2005b. "Speaker: Design around Store Brand." *Supermarket News* 37: 21.

Mudry, Jessica. 2006. "Quantifying an American Eater." *Food, Culture and Society* 9(1): 49–67.

Mudry, Jessica. 2009. *Measured Meals: Nutrition in America*. New York: State University of New York Press.

Murcott, Anne. 1983. "Cooking and the Cooked: A Note on the Domestic Preparation of Meals." In *The Sociology of Food and Eating*, ed. Anne Murcott. Aldershot: Gower.

Nelson, Julie. 1993. "The Study of Choice or the Study of Provisioning? Gender and the Definition of Economics." In *Beyond Economic Man: Feminist Theory and Economics*, ed. Marianne A. Ferber and Julie A. Nelson, 23–26. Chicago: University of Chicago Press.

Nelson, Stephanie. 2007a. "A New Year Means New Savings on Groceries." Accessed April 12, 2007. http://abcnews.go.com/GMA/Consumer/story?id=2860304.

Nelson, Stephanie. 2007b. "The Coupon Mom's Guide to Cutting Your Grocery Bills in Half." Accessed August 14, 2009. http://www.couponmom.com/tutorials-416.

Nestle, Marion. 2002. *Food Politics*. Berkeley: University of California Press.

"The No-Diet Diet." 2005. *Real Simple*, February. Accessed June 10. http://www.realsimple.com/health/nutrition-diet/your-new-healthy-eating-plan-00000000051189/index.html.

Orloff, Ann Shola. 2002. "Explaining U.S. Welfare Reform: Power, Gender, Race and the U.S. Policy Legacy." *Critical Social Policy* 22(1): 96–118.

Orrange, Robert, Francille M. Firebaugh, and Ramona K.Z. Heck. 2001. "Managing Households." In *It's About Time: Couples and Careers*, ed. Phyllis Moen, 153–87. Ithaca, NY: Cornell University Press.

O'Shea, Michael. 2007. "Food to Keep You Healthy." *Parade Magazine*, June 17: 26.

Padavic, Irene, and Barbara Reskin. 2002. *Women and Men at Work*. 2nd ed. Thousand Oaks, CA: Pine Forge Press.

Parker-Pope, Tara. 2011. "Workplace Cited as New Source of Rise in Obesity." *New York Times*, May 26.

Pollan, Michael. 2007. *The Omnivore's Dilemma*. New York: Penguin Press.

Power, Marilyn. 2004. "Social Provisioning as a Starting Point for Feminist Economics." *Feminist Economics* 10(3): 3–19.

Princen, Thomas. 2005. *The Logic of Sufficiency*. Cambridge, MA: The MIT Press.

Risom, Steve, and Ginny Balkenburgh. 2008. "Consumer Intelligence: Dealing with Feeling." *Progressive Grocer*, May 1.

Roff, Robin Jane. 2007. "Shopping for Change? Neoliberal Activism and the Limits to Eating Non-GMO." *Agriculture and Human Values* 24(4): 511–22.

Roth, Dennis. 2000. "America's Fascination with Nutrition." *Food Review* 23(1): 32.

Sayer, Liana C. 2005. "Gender, Time, and Inequality: Trends in Women's and Men's Paid Work, Unpaid Work, and Free Time." *Social Forces* 84(1): 285–303.

Senauer, B., E. Asp, and J. Kinsey. 1991. *Food Trends and the Changing Consumer*. St. Paul, MN: Egan Press.

Sherman, Arloc. 2011. "Despite Deep Recession and High Unemployment, Government Efforts Prevented Poverty from Rising in 2009, New Census Data Show." Center on Budget and Policy Priorities, January 5. Accessed June 24, 2012. http://www.cbpp.org/cms/index.cfm?fa=view&id=3361.

Silva, Jill Wendholt. 2007. "Less Than $2 a Meal: A Reporter Takes the Food Stamp Challenge." *Kansas City Star*, May 29.

Smith, Dorothy E. 1987. *The Everyday World as Problematic: A Feminist Sociology*. Boston: Northeastern University Press.

Smith, Dorothy E. 1990. *The Conceptual Practices of Power: A Feminist Sociology of Knowledge*. Boston: Northeastern University Press.

Smith, Dorothy E. 1999. *Writing the Social: Critique, Theory and Investigations*. Toronto: University of Toronto Press.

Smith, Dorothy E. 2005. *Institutional Ethnography: A Sociology for People*. Lanham, MD: AltaMira Press.

Stage, Sarah. 1997. "Ellen Richards and the Social Significance of the Home Economics Movement." In *Rethinking Home Economics: Women and the History of a Profession*, ed. Sarah Stage and Virginia B. Vincenti, 15–33. Ithaca, NY: Cornell University Press.

Stamos, Jenny. 2007. "Lose Weight for Good." *Women's Day*, April 17.

Steele, Lori Hall. 2007. "9 Best Ways to Save at the Supermarket." *Women's Day*, June.

Strasser, Susan. 1982. *Never Done: A History of American Housework*. New York: Henry Holt and Company.

Szasz, A. 2007. *Shopping Our Way to Safety: How We Changed from Protecting the Environment to Protecting Ourselves*. Minneapolis: University of Minnesota Press.

TED Conferences. 2010. "Jamie Oliver's TED Prize Wish: Teach Every Child about Food." Accessed March 2010. http://www.ted.com/talks/lang/eng/jamie_oliver.html.

Tossi, Mitra. 2002. "Consumer Spending: An Engine for U.S. Job Growth." *Monthly Labor Review* 125(11): 12–22.

Tronto, Joan C. 2002. "The Nanny Question in Feminism." *Hypatia* 17(2): 34–51.

UCLA Center for Health Policy Research. 2008. "Designed for Disease: The Link Between Local Food Environments and Obesity and Diabetes." Accessed May 2008. http://www.healthpolicy.ucla.edu/pubs/Publication.aspx?pubID=250.

Underhill, Paco. 1999. *Why We Buy: The Science of Shopping*. New York: Simon and Schuster.

United Nations. 1995. *Human Development Report 1995*. Oxford: Oxford University Press.

U.S. Bureau of Labor Statistics. 2006. "American Time Use Survey." Accessed August 2008. http://www.bls.gov/tus/tables/a6_0509.htm.

U.S. Bureau of Labor Statistics. 2008. "Married Parents' Use of Time Summary." Accessed May 2010. http://www.bls.gov/news.release/atus2.nr0.htm.

U.S. Bureau of Labor Statistics. 2009. "Highlights of Women's Earnings in 2009." Accessed September 2010. http://www.bls.gov/cps/cpswom 2009.pdf.

U.S. Department of Agriculture. "Meal Planning and Shopping." Nutrition Services Food Stamp Nutrition Education Program. Accessed June 24, 2012. http://www3.ag.purdue.edu/counties/elkhart/Documents/Participant%20Packet%20Meal%20Plan%202010.pdf.

U.S. Department of Agriculture. 2003. "Food CPI, Prices, and Expenditures: Food and Alcoholic Beverages." Economic Research Service. Accessed June 24, 2012. http://www.ers.usda.gov/briefing/cpifoodandexpenditures/Data/Expenditures_tables/table1.htm.

U.S. Department of Agriculture. 2005. "My Pryamid.gov: Steps to a Healthier You." Accessed August 2005. http://www.choosemyplate.gov/food-groups/downloads/MyPyramid_Getting_Started.pdf.

U.S. Department of Agriculture. 2006. "Expanded Food and Nutrition Education Program Success Stories–Food Resource Management." Accessed October 15, 2006. http://www.csrees.usda.gov/nea/food/efnap/success-foodresource.html.

U.S. Department of Agriculture/ERS. 2009. "Food CPI and Food Expenditures." Accessed December 2011. http://www.ers.usda.gov/briefing/cpifoodandexpenditures/Data/Expenditures_tables/.

U.S. Department of Agriculture. 2010a. "Food CPI and Expenditures." Economic Research Service. Accessed October 29, 2009. http://www.ers.usda.gov/Briefing/CPIFoodAndExpenditures/.

U.S. Department of Agriculture. 2010b. "Food Groups: How Many Vegetables are Needed Daily or Weekly?" Accessed March 20, 2010. http://www.choosemyplate.gov/food-groups/vegetables-amount.html#.

U.S. Department of Agriculture, Food and Nutrition. 2011. "SNAP Monthly Data." Accessed November 2011. http://www.fns.usda.gov/pd/snapmain.htm.

U.S. Department of Health and Human Services. 2005a. "Dietary Guidelines for Americans." Accessed May 11, 2005. http://www.health.gov/DietaryGuidelines/dga2005/document/default.htm.

U.S. Department of Health and Human Services. 2005b. "A Healthier You: My Money-Saving Tips." Accessed May 9, 2007. http://www.health.gov/dietaryguidelines/dga2005/healthieryou/html/tips_money_saving.html.

U.S. Department of Health and Human Services. 2005c. "We Can! Families Finding the Balance: A Parent Handbook." NIH publication No. 05–5273. Accessed November 7, 2007. http://www.nhlbi.nih.gov/health/public/heart/obesity/wecan_mats/parent_hb_en.pdf.

U.S. Department of Health and Human Services. 2006. "My Bright Future: Reaching My Goal With Healthy Grocery Shopping." Accessed February 26, 2008. http://www.hrsa.gov/womenshealth/mybrightfutureadult/tipsheets/5_grocery_shopping.html.

U.S. Department of Health and Human Services. 2010. "Dietary Guidelines for Americans." Accessed March 2011. http://www.health.gov/dietaryguidelines/dga2010/DietaryGuidelines2010.pdf.

U.S. Department of Labor. 2000. Bureau of Labor Statistics. "Changes in Women's Labor Force Participation in the 20th Century." Accessed June 2008. http://www.bls.gov/opub/ted/2000/Feb/wk3/art03.htm.

U.S. Department of Labor. 2007a. "Statistics and Data." Accessed June 15, 2008. http://www.dol.gov/wb/stats/main.htm.

U.S. Department of Labor. 2007b. "Working and Work-related Activities Done by Men and Women in 2007." Accessed July 18, 2008. http://www.bls.gov/tus/current/work.htm#al.

U.S. Department of Labor. 2010. "Women in the Labor Force: A Databook." December, Report 1026. Accessed August 2011. http://www.bls.gov/cps/wlf-databook-2010.pdf.

U.S. Food and Drug Administration. 2006. "Nutrition Facts Label." Accessed August 20, 2008. http://www.fda.gov/Food/ResourcesForYou/Consumers/NFLPM/ucm274593.htm.

U.S. Office of Personnel Management. 1992. *Federal Civilian Workforce Statistics: Demographic Profile of the Federal Workforce*. PSO-OWi-5. Washington, DC: U.S. Government Printing Office.

Vincenti, Virginia B. 1997. "Home Economics Moves into the 21st Century." In *Rethinking Home Economics: Women and the History of a Profession*, ed. Sarah Stage and Virginia B. Vincenti, 301–20. Ithaca, NY: Cornell University Press.

Waring, Marilyn. 1999. *Counting for Nothing: What Men Value and What Women are Worth*. 2nd ed. Toronto: University of Toronto Press.

Weinbaum, Batya, and Amy Bridges. 1976. "The Other Side of the Paycheck." *Monthly Review* 28: 88–103.

Weinstein, Bruce, and Mark Scarbrough. 2007. "10 Shopping Tips for Families." Accessed April 19, 2007. http://www.weightwatchers.com/util/art/index_art.aspx?tabnum=1&art_id=31141&sc=3017.

Wells, David R. 1998. *Consumerism and the Movement of Housewives into Wage Work: The Interaction of Patriarchy, Class, and Capitalism in Twentieth Century America*. Brookfield, VT: Ashgate Publishing.

"Win at the Grocery Game: How to Shop Smarter, Cheaper and Faster." 2006. *Consumer Reports*, October.

Wrigley, Neil, Daniel Warm, Barrie Margetts, and Amanda Whelan. 2002. "Assessing the Impact of Improved Retail Access Diet in a 'Food Desert': A Preliminary Report." *Urban Studies* 39(11): 2061–82.

Zelizer, Viviana A. 2005a. "Culture and Consumption." In *The Handbook of Economic Sociology*, 2nd ed., ed. Neil Smelser and Richard Swedberg, 331–54. Princeton, NJ: Princeton University Press.

Zelizer, Viviana A. 2005b. *The Purchase of Intimacy*. Princeton, NJ: Princeton University Press.

Zimmerman, M. 1955. *The Super Market: A Revolution in Distribution*. New York: McGraw-Hill Book Company.

Zukin, Sharon. 2004. *Point of Purchase: How Shopping Changed American Culture*. New York: Routledge.

Zukin, Sharon, and Jennifer Smith Maguire. 2004. "Consumers and Consumption." *Annual Review of Sociology* 30: 173–97.

Zwiebach, Elliot. 2007. "Food Pyramid Chain to Promote Government Guidelines." *Supermarket News*, August 12. Accessed August 2007. http://www.supermarket-news.com/health_wellness/ar/food_pyramid_chain/index.html.

Zwiebach, Elliot. 2010. "The List Maker." *Supermarket News*, August. Accessed November 23, 2010. http://supermarketnews.com/retail-amp-financial/list-maker.

Index

4-H, 19

Acker, Joan, 82
advertising
  and organizing the shopping trip, 35,
    65–6, 71, 75–7, 80–1,
    107
  influencing purchases, 26–7, 85, 91,
    94, 107
  money spent on, 22, 25–6, 94
  weekly ads, construction of,
    90–2
  see also discourse, consumer
    control; marketing
Agro-food system, 2, 54
  concentration of corporations, 21,
    54
  see also food
Albertsons, 21, 55
American Dietetic Association (ADA),
  54–5, 69, 72
American Home Economics Association, 17–18
  see also Richards, Ellen
American Time Use Survey (ATUS), 14
anxiety
  about food practice, 9, 40, 58, 61,
    63
  about mothering, 64, 109
Atwater, W. O., 19

Bauer, Joy, 56–7
Body Mass Index (BMI), 57–8
Boston School of Housekeeping, 18
  branding, 97–9
breastfeeding, 16
budgeting
  and class, 9, 58, 63–4, 82,
    109
  as part of household labor, 67, 69,
    80, 106
  for grocery shopping, 65, 80
buggy see grocery cart

capitalism
  consumer sovereignty and,
    10, 13, 27–9, 91, 101–3,
    110–11
  non-responsibility, 110–12
  see also economy
child-rearing, 15–17
children
  affecting meal selection, 29, 32, 34,
    58
  contribution to feeding work,
    14, 40
  food preferences, 32, 34,
    108
  messages about shopping with,
    41–3, 106
  provisioning for, 7, 40, 55, 64,
    98
  shopping with, 27, 40, 42, 72
choice
  about food, 1–2, 10, 16–17, 20,
    72, 98
  individual decision-making, 3, 10,
    13, 27–8, 45, 58, 110
community-supported agriculture (CSA),
  62
conflict see discourse, intensive
    mothering; division of labor
consumer
  choice, 3–4, 10, 21, 28, 93
  control discourse, 9–10, 86, 99,
    107
  efficient, 69, 80
  management, 86, 94–6
  purchasing, 20
  science, 19, 53, 106
  sovereignty, 10, 13, 27–9, 91–2,
    101–2, 110–11
  types, 94–5
Consumer Reports, 70–1, 74
convenience
  foods, 26–7, 43–4, 70, 80,
    108

cooking
  and guilt, 78
  and scheduling, 35–6, 75–7, 79, 87, 100
  at home, 2–3, 16, 34, 63, 70
  as gendered labor, 43–4
  economically, 70, 108–9
  healthy meals, 2, 108–9
  skills, 2
  variations of, 18, 32, 34, 62, 99–100
coupons
  as encouraging customer loyalty,
    94–5
  expert advice on using, 70–1
  extreme couponing, 1, 71
  time involved in using, 74–5, 78, 81,
    107–8
  using for economical reasons, 9, 26,
    69, 71, 78, 80–1
customer
  building relationships, 6, 9, 23,
    26–7, 85–8, 93–9, 102
  loyalty cards, 93–5
  service, 23, 25–6, 40, 55, 86–8
  see also advertising; discourse, con-
    sumer control; marketing

Deutsch, Tracy, 24–5, 112
DeVault, Marjorie, 4
  see also Feeding the Family
Dietary Guidelines for Americans, 48,
  54–5
dieticians
  as food experts, 17, 55, 69, 73, 106
  employment as, 19–20, 55
  history of, 54
  see also home economists;
    nutritionists
Direct Store Delivery (DSD), 88
discourse
  competing, 105–10
  consumer control, 9–10, 86, 99,
    106–7
  consumer sovereignty, 27–8, 102
  contradiction between, 10, 59, 64,
    99, 102, 108–10
  definition of, 6
  efficient housewife, 9–10, 59,
    65–81, 102, 106, 108–9
  food marketing, 28, 85–101

institutional, 44
intensive mothering, 109
nutrition, individual responsibility for,
  9–10, 45–63, 65, 102, 106–7,
  110
  see also consumer; efficiency;
    nutrition
division of labor
  in food system, 19–20
  negotiating household, 37–40, 106,
    111
domestic workers, 15

early buying allowance, 92
eating out
  as convenience, 33, 44, 76, 100
  as less healthy, 57
  related to income, 32, 40, 79
  underreporting of, 76
economy
  consumption, 13
  definition of, 111
  gendered, 110–12
  social organization of, 109–10
  see also capitalism, market
efficiency
  and convenience, 43–4, 70–1, 108
  and discipline, 76, 81, 108
  discourse, 10, 59, 64, 67–74, 76,
    80–2, 102, 106, 108–9
  household, 18
  movement, 18–19
  skills, 79, 108
  strategies, 73, 76, 78, 82, 109–10
  see also discourse, efficient
    housewife
Expanded Food and Nutrition Education
  Program (EFNEP), 79–80
experts
  food, 13, 17–20, 45–6, 53
  nutrition, 54, 56, 59, 60
  on grocery shopping, 69–70, 72–4
  on mothering, 97
  related to discourses, 61, 69
Extreme Couponing, 71

family see division of labor, household
  production, motherhood
family and consumer science, 19, 53

farmer's market, 2–3, 20, 41, 62–3,
    101, 108–9
Fast Food Nation, 2
Feeding the Family, 4, 31
food
  allergy, 36
  cost
    for healthy items, 59, 63, 108
    in varying stores, 22
    with children, 7
    within budget, 9, 67, 70, 74
  meals
    from fast food restaurants, 55, 76
    healthy, 2, 46, 57, 100, 108
    home-cooked, 2–3, 16, 57, 81
    planning, 18, 32–4, 36–7, 40,
      43–4, 66–7, 69, 76, 80, 82, 106
    preparation service, 99–100
    scheduling, 32, 34, 35, 70, 79,
      100, 106
  movements, 16 -17, 63
  preparation
    as prepackaged, 9, 20, 44, 81,
      99–100
    provisioning, definition of, 32
    to make healthy meals, 57
    to make household meals, 4, 32,
      34–5, 39, 57, 61, 75
    see also grocery shopping
  purchases
    as organizations, 7
    by households, 7, 65, 112
    for children, 43, 64
    impulse, 25, 70, 72
    monitoring by stores, 95–6
    retail influences in, 10, 17, 25–6,
      74, 93, 107
    unnecessary, 9, 90
  pyramid, 27, 48, 54–5, 62, 69
  stamps, 78–80, 109
  see also community-supported
    agriculture; locavore
Food, Inc.
  movie, 2
  website, 2
Food and Drug Administration (FDA),
  51–2, 54, 64
Food Marketing Institute (FMI), 8, 28,
  86

Food Show, 8, 86, 92–3
Food Stamp Challenge, 80
Frederick, Christine, 18
  see also scientific management

gardening, 17
Good Housekeeping, 8, 47, 56
Good Morning America, 8, 47
government
  as institution, 5, 10–11
  deregulation, 4, 21
  role in nutrition, 63–4, 83, 106
grocery cart, 23, 26, 40, 42–3, 73
Grocery Manufacturers of America, 26,
  86, 97
  see also Willis, Paul
grocery shopping
  and children, 7, 14, 34, 42, 60, 64,
    72, 76–7, 106
  as work, 3–4, 7, 9–10, 14, 31–45,
    79, 81, 102, 106
  at mom and pop stores, 22–4
  as unpaid labor, 4, 7, 10, 15, 106,
    111
  conceptualization of, 4
  work of
    as efficiency strategy, 82
    as household management, 18,
      69, 73–4
    budgeting, 77, 80, 106
    for meals at home, 3–4, 43–4
    lists, 33–9, 43, 65–7, 69–70, 74,
      76, 81, 106
    looking at ads, 35, 65–6, 71,
      75–7, 80–1
    planning, 32–7, 50, 65–7, 74–6,
      102, 106
    related to employment status,
      14–15, 34, 36, 43, 100,
      108
    scheduling, 32, 35–6, 40
    with versus without children, 40
  time spent
    full-time versus part-time, 36, 41,
      44, 63, 75, 109
    in relation to money spent, 90,
      102
    in the store, 41, 43, 66–7, 70,
      73–5, 80–1

taking the place of other events, 100
with or without children, 72, 76
see also food, provisioning; work
Gross Domestic Product (GDP), 28, 109
Guthman, Julie, 3

health
as a lifestyle, 8, 11, 16, 38–9, 41, 49, 52–56, 95
and nutrition, 8, 45–6, 54, 56
grade cards, 64
in regard to children, 15–16, 17, 39, 46, 57, 61–2, 97
in relationship to cost, 59, 108
in relationship to food choices, 7, 9–10, 47, 52–3, 55, 97
in relationship to meals, 2, 57, 107
issues, 33, 48, 53
Health, 73
home economics, 17–20, 67
see also consumer, science; family
home economists, 17, 19
household
division of labor, 37–40, 106, 111
unpaid labor, 4, 10, 15, 106
see also grocery shopping
housewife, efficient, 9, 65–83, 106–7
Hy-Vee, 55, 81

impulse buying
by partners, 38
in relation to self-service, 25
strategies to encourage, 10, 83, 93, 102, 107–8
using lists to prevent, 70, 81
with children, 72–3
withstanding, 69–70, 73, 81
individualization, 110
institutional ethnography
knowledge, 47
research method, 5–8, 105–6
relations of ruling, 82
social organization, 9–10
intensive mothering, 15–16, 64, 109, 111

Kansas State University
College of Human Ecology, 19

labor, division of
household, 15, 17, 37–40, 106, 111
land-grant universities, 19, 53
Lempert, Phil, 69–70, 73
Let's Move, 1, 57
see also Obama, Michelle
locavore, 3

Maniates, Michael, 110
manufacturers, 2, 21, 25–6, 29, 71, 86–8, 91–4, 96, 102–3, 107, 111
market, 13, 25, 27
see also capitalism; consumer, sovereignty; neoliberalism
marketing
discourse, 85–6, 93–9, 107
history, 25–7
managers, practice of, 88–90
strategy, 94–6
to the public
to children, 98
to environmentally conscious shoppers, 97–8
to mothers, 97
see also advertising, branding
meal preparation, 2–3, 14, 35, 99–100
More, 8, 47
motherhood *see* anxiety, breastfeeding, child-rearing, intensive mothering, standard North American family
MyPlate, 50
MyPyramid, 48–9, 55

National Center on Addiction and Substance Abuse, 57
Nelson, Stephanie, 69, 71–2
neoliberalism, 4, 10, 28, 109, 111
see also consumer, sovereignty; market
New England Kitchen, 18
nutrition
calories, 19, 47–9, 50, 52–3, 60, 107
carbohydrates, 9, 19, 52, 107

constituent parts
discourse, 10, 45–63
facts label, 51–2
fats, 3, 9, 19, 49–50, 52, 54–6
knowledge, 47–53
policy, 53–4
protein, 19, 50, 53, 56, 61
reductionism, 48
see also food; MyPlate; MyPyramid
nutritionists, 19–20, 45, 54, 69, 106

Obama, Michelle, 1, 3, 57
obesity, 1–2, 11, 57, 98, 110
Oliver, Jamie, 1–2
Omnivore's Dilemma, The, 2
see also Pollan, Michael

Parade Magazine, 56
Personal Responsibility and Work
    Opportunity Act, 109
planning, 18, 32–7, 39–40, 69–74
Piggly Wiggly, 22
Pollan, Michael, 2–3, 110
see also Omnivore's Dilemma, The
price
    and consumer demand, 27, 87–8
    as the focus of retail, 25, 91, 94, 102
    buying items at full versus sale, 67,
        71, 75, 108
    comparing, 74–5, 80–1, 109
    determining food choice, 77
    in limiting discretionary purchases,
        82–3
    in relation to different stores, 22, 24
    of healthier foods, 59, 61–2, 96–7,
        108
    rising, 105
    unit, 74
Price is Right, The, 87
product placement, 85, 88–90
product mark-up, 92
Progressive Grocer, 8, 86
Promise Institute, 54–5

race
    cooking and serving in restaurants, 15
    in this study, 111
    rise of chain stores, 24–5

Real Simple, 8, 70
recession, effects of, 15, 105–6
recipes, 32, 37, 59, 101
restaurants *see* eating out
retail
    concentration, 21
    environment, 4, 8, 10, 26, 29, 44,
        82, 86–7
    managers, 5, 8–10, 24, 44, 74, 83,
        85–94, 101–3, 106–7
    market, 3–4, 7, 13, 21, 94, 99
    promotions, 85, 93–7, 107–8
    sales clerks, 23–6
    strategies, 3, 10–11, 26, 73–4, 89,
        95–6, 108
Richards, Ellen, 17–18
    see also Boston School of
        Housekeeping

sales clerks, 23–6
sales representatives, 88–9
Saunders, Clarence, 22
Schlosser, Eric, 2
    see also Fast Food Nation
scientific management, 18
    see also Frederick, Christine; Taylor,
        Frederick
self-service, 22, 25–7, 29
signage, 85, 89–90, 92, 95, 98, 102,
    107
Simple Living, 8, 47
Slow Food, 16, 63
slotting fees, 26, 88
Smith, Dorothy E.
    institutional ethnography, 5–6,
        106
    on discourse and social organization,
        6, 15
social class
    and economy, 82
    constraints of provisioning, 18–19,
        59, 61, 63, 64, 82, 109, 111
    makeup of study, 106
    related to discourse, 9, 45, 58, 61,
        64
social organization of food system,
    2–3, 5, 10, 62, 75–6, 81
standardization, 19

K634

standard North American family, 15, 82, 111
state, 3–4, 21, 79, 109–11
  see also government
supercenter, definition of, 21
  hypermarket, 22
supermarket
  definition of, 20–1
  design, 6, 22–5, 85
  retail consolidation, 21
  square footage, 22
  strategy, 13, 73, 85, 98, 101, 111
Supermarket News, 8, 86, 101, 107
Supplemental Nutrition Assistance
  Program (SNAP), 83, 105

Taste of Home, 59
Taylor, Frederick, 18
  see also scientific management
Technology, Entertainment, Design
  (TED), 1
Temporary Assistance to Needy Families (TANF), 83
text
  connection to discourse, 5–6, 9, 26,
    47, 67
  definition, 6
  examples of, used in study, 8, 44–5,
    67, 90–1
Today Show, The, 8, 47, 56, 69

Unilever, 54–5, 94
United States Department of

Agriculture, 8, 19, 20, 48, 50, 53,
  56, 63
  expanded Food and Nutrition Pro-
    gram, 79–80
  Health and Human Services, 8,
    47–8, 49, 52–3, 64, 69
    see also MyPyramid
  Labor, 14

Wall Street Journal, The, 9, 86
Walmart, 21, 23, 46, 59–60, 77, 82,
  87, 97
Weight Watchers, magazine, 8, 73–4
Weight Watchers, program, 8, 55–6
Wendy's, 55
Whole Foods Market, 3–4, 21
Willis, Paul, 26
  see also Grocery Manufacturers of
    America
Women, Infants and Children (WIC),
  83
Women's Day, 71–2
work
  and gendered division of labor, 4,
    15, 17
  effects of employment on provision-
    ing, 4, 10, 22, 77, 82, 106,
    108–11
  paid, 15, 19, 111–12
  unpaid, 4, 10, 13–15, 106, 111
  women's increased participation in
    paid, 14, 19
World War II, 6, 22, 83